Intermediate Shotokan Karate

Unravelling the Brown Belt and First Black Belt Kata

ASHLEY CROFT

THE CROWOOD PRESS

First published in 2009 by
The Crowood Press Ltd
Ramsbury, Marlborough
Wiltshire SN8 2HR

www.crowood.com

British Library Cataloguing-in-Publication Data
A catalogue record for this book is available from the British Library.

ISBN 978 1 84797 078 7

Disclaimer
Please note that the author and the publisher of this book are not
responsible in any manner whatsoever for any damage or injury of any
kind that may result from practising, or applying, the principles, ideas,
techniques and/or following the instructions/information described in
this publication. Since the physical activities described in this book may
be too strenuous in nature for some readers to engage in safely, it is
essential that a doctor be consulted before undertaking training.

Photography by Martin Baugh.

Typeset by Jean Cussons Typesetting, Diss, Norfolk
Printed and bound in Singapore by Craft Print International Ltd.

Contents

Dedication

I would like to dedicate this book to the Black Belts of the Chiltern Karate Association for their support over the years. Many of them have become good friends. I have also enjoyed instructing them, which has undoubtedly assisted my own self-development.

Acknowledgements

I would like to offer special thanks to Craig Jones, Erin Thwaites and Robin Thwaites, who all assisted me with the bunkai (applications) demonstrated within this book. I would also like to thank Sensei Rick Clark (8th Dan) and Sensei Patrick McCarthy (8th Dan) for their inspiration and for opening my mind to the wider aspects of the martial arts.

Last but not least, I would like to thank Martin Baugh for his expert advice and hard work taking the photographs included within the book.

Intermediate Shotokan Karate

Unravelling the Brown Belt and First Black Belt Kata

1 Introduction

The kata provide a means through which to practise the myriad of karate techniques with full speed, power, kime and correct breathing. When performed correctly and at high speed, there is no need to pull the techniques or hold back in any way, which is often the case with partner work for fear of causing injury. It is for this reason kata practice should be an integral part of any training regime; if each move is performed in the right way and with precision, the benefits of kata practice are substantial.

Sensei Richard Kim said, when emphasizing the importance of kata training, 'Kata are the heart of karate and it is on kata that karate is based. Karate without the kata is not karate.' Sensei Kim was of the firm view that there can be no karate without the serious practice and study of the kata. This is also a view held by the famous masters of the past. Kata were the main method of training for the likes of Masters Matsumura, Itosu, Azato and the father of modern-day karate, Master Gichin Funakoshi. But the reality today is often found to be to the contrary. In many dojo, kata are relegated to the position of being regarded as necessary but unimportant and certainly subordinate to kumite (sparring). The kata, in effect, are being practised merely as a set of calisthenics without real commitment or sense of purpose.

When exploring the possible reasons why this position has evolved, it becomes clear that there has been a lack of understanding as to what the kata really represent; that is, the self-defence themes contained within them and the benefits of serious practice. This is not intended to be a criticism of any one instructor, but a consequence of events and how karate has evolved over the last 100 years. When karate was exported to Japan the kata underwent significant changes and it appears that by the time Sensei Nakayama was head of the Japan Karate Association (JKA), little or no emphasis was being placed on meaningful kata bunkai (application principles). This rapid evolution was commented on by Sensei Shigeru Egami (Nakayama's successor at the JKA) in his book *The Heart of Karate-do*, in which he made the following comment about the development of kata in his time: 'Even in the forty years I have been practising, the changes have been many. It would be interesting to be able to go back in time, to the point when the kata were created and study them.'

The aim of this book is to build on the Taikyoku and Heian kata, which are foundation kata and are covered in a previous book by the author: Shotokan Karate – Unravelling the Kata (published by The Crowood Press, 2006). The kata covered in the following pages are the intermediate and more advanced kata required for advancement through the Brown Belts to the Coveted Shodan – Black Belt 1st Dan.

Remember when practising or learning a new kata there are no secrets to the individual moves which in isolation are all basic to learn. The difficulty comes when putting all the moves together in sequence to form the pattern that makes up the kata.

When studying the kata, it is essential that it is understood that the offensive and defensive moves were not created for defence against the modern karate techniques that are delivered from a long stance and from a distance, but rather from close quarters. For this reason, all the applications in this book commence from the close-quarter fighting position. It should also be understood that in addition to the obvious kicks, blocks and strikes, the kata also include grappling techniques, locks, vital-point strikes, throwing techniques, chokes and strangleholds. In respect of the throwing techniques, karate students often dismiss these as not relevant or part of karate – they are for the judoka and not for them. This is, however, far from the truth. Master Gichin Funakoshi has an interesting few lines in his book *Karate Do Kyohan* which serve to put the record straight: 'Throwing techniques include byobudaoshi, komanage, kubiwa, katawaguruma, tsubamegaeshi, yaridama, taniotoshi, udewa, sakatsuchi and others. All these techniques should be studied, referring to basic kata.' Please therefore study the kata with an open mind and employ some lateral thinking. Closed minds will prevent serious advancement.

2 The History and Evolution of Karate

Whilst modern-day karate is generally considered to be Japanese, it was in fact imported into Japan from the small island of Okinawa during the early part of the twentieth century, when it incorporated the Japanese customs and traditions that are such an integral part of karate today and which give it the perceived Japanese origin. Okinawa is the main island of the Ryukyu Archipelago, a string of islands located in the East China Sea, approximately 500 miles (800km) to the south of Japan. Remarkably for its size – having a total land area of 870 sq miles (1,256sq km) – Okinawa has had a major influence on the 'Japanese' martial arts as we know them today.

Okinawa Karate Schools

Various systems of indigenous martial arts have been practised in Okinawa for centuries and were historically referred to simply as 'Toudi', 'Tode' or just 'Te'. The word 'Te' translates literally as 'hands'. It is known that over the years these various systems developed into three distinct styles around the main towns of Naha, Shuri and Tomari, after which they were named. The system of 'Te' from Naha became known simply as Naha-te (hands of Naha), while those of Shuri and Tomari became known as Shuri-te and Tomari-te, respectively. The use of the term 'karate' ('empty hand') to encompass all these indigenous arts is relatively recent, being agreed at a meeting in Okinawa of prominent martial arts masters in 1936.

While it is fair to assume that there would have been many different karate schools within the Naha region, it has been established that Naha-te

was developed into Gojo Ryu (the hard and soft school), under the leadership of two prominent masters, Kanryo Higaonna (1840–1910) and Chojun Miyagi (1888–1953). Gojo Ryu is how it is still known today. In the late nineteenth century Shuri-te and Tomari-te merged, taking the name of Shorin Ryu (flexible pine school). It is from Shorin Ryu that Shotokan was established by Master Gichin Funakoshi (1868–1957) and from which Shotokai and Wado Ryu karate have evolved. A further style, named Shito Ryu, was also developed by Master Mabuni Kenwa (1889–1952) and is widely practised in Okinawa today. Shito Ryu is a combination of the three

Fig. 1 Okinawa and the East China Sea region.

9

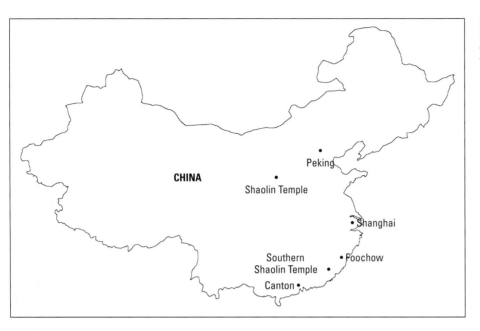

Fig. 2 The location of the Shaolin Temple.

ancient arts of Naha-te, Shuri-te and Tomari-te and also includes the use of weapons such as the bo (wooden staff) and sai (three-pronged truncheon). Master Mabuni Kenwa was a student of both Anko Itosu of Shuri-te lineage and Kanryo Higaonna of Naha-te lineage. This is reflected in the name he gave to his style, Shito Ryu, in which 'Shi' derives from the Japanese pronunciation for 'Ito' in 'Itosu' and 'To' from the Japanese pronunciation for 'Higa' in 'Higaonna'.

Despite the three labels being assigned to the Okinawan styles of 'Te', there has always been some overlap among them and this is still evident today in the practice of kata. For example, the kata Hengetsu (original name Seishan) originates from Naha-te, but is practised by Shotokan and Wado Ryu. The Tekki kata (original name Naihanchi) was practised equally by Naha-te and Shuri-te and is now one of the cornerstones of Shotokan karate.

The Shaolin Temple and the Chinese Connection

Closer examination of the roots of karate reveals an interesting link with the martial arts that have flourished in China for centuries. The most famous school of Chinese martial arts is Shaolin Quan which originates from the world-renowned Shaolin Temple.

The Shaolin Temple was first constructed in 495AD by order of the Northern Wei Emperor Xiao Wendi for an Indian monk named Batuo, as a place where he and his disciples could translate Buddhist scriptures and other texts from Sanskrit into Chinese. It also served as a base from which to preach and transmit Buddhism further.

The place chosen for the temple was the western foothills of the Songshan Mountains, which are located in the central China plains, 8 miles (13km) north-west of the city of Dengfeng, in what is now Henan Province. The position chosen was very strategic. The central China plains are located between the Yellow (Huanye) River to the north and the Hanjiang River to the south. Approximately 50 miles (80km) to the north-west of the Songshan Mountain range is Luoyang, which was Xiao Wendi's capital. Luoyang has often been chosen by the Chinese emperors as their seat of power and is frequently referred to in Chinese history as the eastern capital. To the east of the mountains is the ancient city of Kaifeng (Bianliang). Whoever controlled Songshan controlled the ancient roadway between Kaifeng and Luoyang and also to other surrounding Provinces, making it of strategic military importance. Even today the positional importance of Henan can be seen; it is centrally placed and surrounded by the six Provinces of Hubei, Shaanxi, Shanxi, Hebei, Shandong and Anhui.

There is evidence to indicate that martial arts were introduced to the Shaolin Temple very soon after the temple was constructed in 495AD. By the end of the Northern Wei Dynasty (386–534), a number of the monks were proficient in some form of fighting art. Written descriptions of early Shaolin martial arts depict it as an art that contained grappling, throws, joint locks, kicks and punches.[1] It is suggested that one of the driving forces for this was the need to provide security for the temple property against attack from bandits and rebellious farmers. There is evidence from early inscriptions on stone stele at the Shaolin Temple that bandits and wild animals roamed freely around the surrounding area. China was certainly undergoing a period of instability at this time, which would have required the temple to have a protection force. In the Northern Wei Dynasty there was frequent conflict between the ruling and working classes. The monks of the Shaolin Temple would possibly have been associated with the ruling classes because of the growing wealth of the temple under the protection of the royal court. Written records from the Northern Qi Dynasty describe the Shaolin monks as being able to lift hundreds of kilograms and being very good at boxing and horse-riding.

The Shaolin Temple became a centre of excellence for the fighting arts, with martial artists from across China making a pilgrimage to the temple to practise with the monk soldiers. The consequential cross-fertilization of martial arts ideas, techniques and philosophies between the Shaolin Temple masters and outsiders influenced many of the Chinese martial arts styles we see today and those from other Asian countries.

The Southern Shaolin Temple

While the Shaolin Temple is world-renowned, what is not common knowledge is that there was more than one temple; at one point during the Yuan Dynasty there were at least five further temples linked to the main Shaolin Temple in Songshan. While martial arts may have been practised at each of these temples, the one that emerges as most prominent in this respect is the southern Shaolin Temple. The existence of a southern Shaolin Temple had for years been doubted and its supposed location shrouded in mystery, to the extent that it was considered folklore rather than reality. It has, however, now been concluded that it probably did exist and was located high in the Diayun Mountain range adjacent to the village of Lin Shan on the Jiu Lian Peak (Nine Lotus Peak). This is approximately 8 miles (13km) to the west of the city of Pu Tian within the eastern Fujian Province.

On 18 September 1990 the Chinese Government permitted excavation of the site and significant archaeological discoveries were made. The excavations were undertaken by archaeologists on behalf of the Putian museum. The area excavated covered 1,196sq yd (1,000sq m) and unearthed brickwork from the Tang, Song, Yuan, Ming and Qing Dynasties. A pagoda tablet was found with the name of the monk Zhen Yue, who died in 504 during the Northern Dynasty period (386–581). It was concluded that a temple of sorts existed on the site from the time of the Northern Dynasty through to the Qing Dynasty. From pottery finds the archaeologists were able to establish that the temple was called Lin Quang. The village adjacent to the temple is called Lin Shan and within the area of Lin Shan there are a small number of other temples that actually record connections with the Shaolin Temple and consider themselves to be associate or subordinate temples of Lin Quang.

Although circumstantial, the decline of Lin Quang Temple appears to coincide with the reported demise of the southern Shaolin Temple. It is said that during the Qing Dynasty monks of the southern Shaolin Temple conspired with other people from the Han race to overthrow the Dynasty resulting in the destruction of the temple. Legend states that at the rear of the southern Shaolin Temple there was a hall called Red Flower Pavilion where the monks and co-conspirators swore their allegiance and plotted the demise of the Qing Dynasty.

Fig. 3 Famous main gate of the Shaolin Temple.

The archaeological discoveries at Lin Shan enable the conclusion to be drawn that there was at least some martial training taking place there during its history. One of the finds was large stone stele on which is carved 'this temple's martial monks Yong Qi and Jin Qi built a trough in September 1063'. Also discovered at the site were rusty weapons of various description and other items that are purportedly training aids used by the resident monk soldiers. There were also other archaeological finds that date the central temple building back to 557 in the Tang Dynasty,[2] which is only sixty-one years after the construction of the northern Shaolin Temple in Songshan.

The Chinese Government has now officially recognized this location as the probable location of the southern Shaolin Temple and recently reconstructed a new temple on the original site with the intention of it again becoming a regional centre of excellence for martial arts. There is, however, still some dispute in academic circles in China that this is the actual location of a 'Shaolin' temple, with other sites being proposed as possibilities. One such site is located just north of the city of Quanzhou in the Qing Yuan Mountains. This area is named as the location of the southern Shaolin Temple in a Qing Dynasty record entitled *Records of the Western Mountain*, which was compiled during the reign of Emperor Dao Guang (1821–50). A different location for

the temple is recorded in the *Three Mountain Record* revised in 1182 by Liang Ke Jia, who was from the city of Quanzhou. Volume 36 is called *Fuqing County Temples* and within it there is an entry that states that the Dong Lin Temple in Xin Ning is in the same area as the Shaolin Yuan. The existence of a Shaolin Temple in the Fuqing area is also recorded in the *Records of the Min Area* dated to around 1499. These record that there are eight temples in the Xin Ning area of Fuqing County: Fang Dong, Dong Lin, Hou Tang, Long Xi, Zhao Fu, Long Ju, Shaolin and Da Xu.[3] During the Yuan Dynasty it was also reported that martial arts were flourishing at the Kai Yuan Temple in Quanzhou where the famous Shaolin monk Xiaoshan spent a number of years.

Regardless of where the temple was actually located, the legend surrounding it states that the fifth Abbot of the Northern (Songshan) Shaolin Temple had two special disciples who were adept martial artists. One disciple remained at Songshan while he dispatched the other to the Fujian Province to establish a second Shaolin Temple. From this point on, the temple played an important role in the development and evolution of martial arts within the southern and eastern areas of China.

It was also said that during the Ming Dynasty (1368–1644) a Shaolin monk named Yi Fa often visited the Shaolin Temple in Quanzhou and he later settled there and became the abbot. During his time there he extended the temple and passed on Shaolin martial arts to the monks.[4]

It is recorded that the monks of the southern Shaolin Temple were often called into service by the emperor in the battle against Japanese pirates that plagued China's eastern coastal region in the sixteenth century. In particular, in 1522 during the reign of Emperor Jiajing, the monks of the southern Shaolin Temple won a reputation by driving out the pirates who were constantly sending raiding parties into the coastal areas of Jiansu, Zhejiang and Fujian Provinces.

Evolution of Chinese Martial Arts

There is a saying in China, first quoted in a

famous book of the Qing Dynasty, *Jian Hu Ji*, that 'all martial arts under heaven originate from Shaolin'. While this reflects a widely held belief that many of the martial arts as we know them today originated from the Shaolin Temple, it is actually an overly romantic view. It is now almost universally acknowledged that martial arts in China pre-date the construction of the Shaolin Temple, but the saying, in wide use throughout China, does give an indication of the high regard in which the Shaolin Temple is held and an indication of the influence that it has had on the evolution of martial arts in China and indeed across the whole of the Far East. There are proven historical links between the martial arts masters from within the Shaolin Temple and masters from not only Japan but other Asian countries such as Korea, Taiwan, Vietnam and Singapore.

China has a long tradition of martial arts, both weapon-based and barehanded. It is, however, impossible to establish with certainty the exact development of the martial arts in China, although various archaeological excavations and ancient writings provide some historical signposts that help in this quest. Ancient relics indicate that the Chinese have been practising systemized physical exercise to limber up for around 10,000 years[5] and according to Chinese mythology the earliest forms of discernible martial arts started to appear during the era of Huangdi (the Yellow Emperor) who is said to have reigned from 2698 to 2599BC.[6] Huangdi was a soldier rising to the rank of general before becoming emperor. As emperor, he wrote a number of treatises on medicine, astrology and martial arts and credited to him is the *Huangdi Neijing Suwen* (*The Yellow Emperor's Manual of Corporeal Medicine*), which is the earliest Chinese medical writing.[7] In the *Records of the Grand Historian*, written between 109–91BC, it is recorded that Huangdi trained his soldiers to use weapons, suggesting a deliberate and systemized approach to military preparedness. He also allegedly created the art of Jiao Di (horn-butting), which was a crude form of wrestling practised by soldiers. This was said to have been used in practice before battle, with soldiers wearing horns on their heads as a sign of courage, then using them

to butt each other in an organized contest.[8] Jiao Di developed into a style of wrestling known as Jiao Li, which included strikes, throws, joint manipulation and pressure-point strikes. The earliest graphic descriptions of this wrestling are to be found on bones, tortoise shells and bronze objects of the Shang Dynasty (1700–1100BC), vividly portraying wrestlers grappling together. Writings on the subject can be traced back to the period of Western Zhou (1100–771BC), for example: 'In early winter … the emperor ordered his generals to study military arts and practise shooting, charioteering and Jiao Li.' Jiao Li was listed as a military sport alongside archery and chariot racing[9] and was recorded in the *Classic of Rites*, an ancient text compiled during the Warring States period (475BC to 221BC), in which encouragement was given to the 'practise of pugilism, archery and wrestling'.[10]

In ancient China there also existed a form of fighting called 'Leitai' or 'fighting on the platform'. The word Leitai means 'beat [a drum] platform' and refers to the raised platform that would form the fighting ring similar to boxing of today, but without the ropes. Leitai dates back to the Zhou Dynasty and was a combination of wrestling and boxing, with weapons being permitted on occasion. Bouts were almost gladiatorial in nature, with the winner being declared the 'platform-occupier' and retaining the title until he was beaten, incapacitated or thrown from the platform by a challenger. Fatal injuries were not uncommon. A Leitai competition would go on until no more challenges were made to an occupier, who was then declared the champion.

According to *The Book of Zhuang Zi*, by the end of the Spring, Autumn and Warring States periods (770–22 BC) unarmed combat had become a highly developed skill with many methods of attack, defence, counter-attack and feints.[11] *The Book of Zhuang Zi* is a Daoist (Taoist) book covering the psychology and practice of martial arts written by an author of the same name, Zhuang Zi, who is believed to have lived in the fourth century BC. In another ancient book called *Shih Ching* (also known as the Book of Songs), which is the earliest collection of Chinese poems written circa 600BC, it is stated 'without fighting arts there would be no courage to speak of'. During the Warring States period, boxing matches were also popular and became very common among the rank and file with large audiences in attendance.[12]

Further evidence of early martial arts practice is recorded on stone carvings of the Han Dynasty (206BC– 220AD) found in the Nanyang region of Henan Province. A museum dedicated to these carvings has been built near to the site and holds a collection of over 1,300 stone carvings dated between 206BC–220AD. Some of the carvings depict a variety of martial arts activities including fencing, archery, grappling with wild animals and unarmed combat. In one depiction a man is shown attacking with his spear while his adversary is defending unarmed.[13] The early use of martial arts is also depicted on a fresco of a Han period tomb excavated in Dahuting, Mixian County. It is entitled *Sumo* and was painted 300 years before the construction of the Shaolin Temple.[14] In the fresco there are two figures facing each other in a fighting posture waiting for the opportunity to strike. There were two other types of martial art that appeared during the Han Dynasty. One was known as Shoubo ('barehand exercise') and the other Jiandao ('sword play').[15] The *History of the Han Dynasty* also contains chapters on fencing, unarmed combat and archery.[16]

During these ancient times the weapon-based systems were being systematically developed. Between the sixteenth and eleventh centuries BC the Bronze Age gave rise to the creation of an array of weapons, including various designs of spears, swords, halberds and axes. These weapons required a corresponding development in the skill needed to wield them and competitions started to develop. Injuries during these competitions were frequent and in one fencing competition in the state of Zhao more than sixty people were killed or injured over a period of seven days. By the Qin Dynasty (221–207BC) the contests were becoming more and more rule-bound with referees being used. In 1975, during the excavation of a Qin Dynasty tomb in Jiangling, Hubei Province, archaeologists unearthed a wooden comb which had a colour painting on it depicting a wrestling match. The contestants are bare-chested, wearing what appear to be shorts with belts around their waists, while a third man acts as referee.[17]

Archery has a long history in China. As far back as the Western Zhou Dynasty (1100BC–771BC) archery and chariot racing was practised as a sport.[18] King Wuling of the State of Zhao in the Warring States period (475BC–221BC) established a cavalry in 471BC and shooting arrows from the back of galloping horses became one of the important combat skills for the army, similar to the samurai art of Yabusame, which also involved archery whilst on horseback. During the Tang Dynasty (618–907AD) horsemen's archery became one of the imperial examinations.

A famous Chinese physician and surgeon by the name of Hua Tuo lived during the three kingdoms period (220–280AD). He was proficient in the use of acupuncture and is believed to be the first doctor in the world to use general anaesthesia. As well as being a skilled surgeon, Hua Tuo developed physiotherapy and a system of physical exercises known as Wu Qin Xi, which consisted of movements imitating five animals, the tiger, the bear, the deer, the monkey and the crane. His system resembled shadow boxing and was used primarily to promote health. The mimicking of animal movements features predominantly in Chinese martial arts systems – styles have developed from animals such as the tiger, panther, leopard and bear, as well as styles mimicking the actions of birds such as the eagle, crane and chicken. Styles also emerged using insect movements, for example the praying mantis, while others use the snake and dragon as a source of inspiration. The reason for imitating the fighting techniques of animals came from observing them fighting and seeing that they possessed the natural talents required to survive in a competitive environment.[19] Dr Jwing-Ming Yang has calculated that since ancient times there have probably been more than 5,000 martial arts styles created in China. Over time the less effective styles have died out, leaving a smaller number that have been tried and tested in anger and found to be effective. Even today, it is reported that more than a thousand different styles exist.[20]

The Dunhuang Grottoes (also known the Mogao Grottoes) in Gansu Province consist of 480 caverns and 59,800sq yd (50,000sq m) of murals providing an amazing insight into all aspects of ancient life in China. Many scenes in the murals, painted over a 1,000-year period from the fourth to fourteenth centuries, are about wrestling.[21] One 22yd (20m) long fresco painted in the Northern Zhou Dynasty (557–81) is composed of six pictures about life of Buddha's; It describes a bout of xiangpu between two contestants overseen by a referee. Xiangpu closely resembles modern day Japanese sumo. In a grotto built in the Five Dynasties period (907–60) there is another wall painting depicting xiangpu. The competitors are dressed in gowns and performing on a carpet or mat to provide a competition area. In the court of the Qing Dynasty (1644–1911) there were special 'xiangpu camps', at which imperial guards were trained in wrestling, archery, horsemanship and other martial arts. In the Manchu language the wrestlers in a xiangpu camp were called bukus and were classified into grades according to their skill in a tournament held twice a year. Aside from taking part collectively in training camps, xiangpu wrestlers often worked privately to develop their skills in secret.[22]

Chinese Martial-Art Links with Okinawa

There is a clear link between the Chinese and Okinawan martial arts dating back to at least the fourteenth century, when in 1393 a Chinese community of administrators and craftsmen settled on Okinawa at the direction of the Chinese Government. The records refer to these early settlers as 'Sanjuroku Seito', which translates as 'the thirty-six families'. This original title stuck and is the name by which they became popularly known. The purpose of the settlement was to promote relations between the two countries and as such it served as an arrival point for Chinese diplomats and traders for many years to follow. The settlement was located in the Kume (original name Kuninda) area of Naha and also became known as Kumemura. Oral tradition

Fig. 4   Xiangpu wrestlers c.220AD.

states that the thirty-six families were responsible for initiating the spread of the Chinese martial art of Ch'uan fa (literally 'way of the fist') throughout Okinawa. Other records refer to this group as the 'hundred names of China' and perhaps more importantly as 'the thirty-six families of Fukien'. This provides a direct link between the settlement and the Fukien Province on the east coast of China, home of the southern Shaolin Temple.

The Chinese influence was not restricted to the settlement in Kume. There is evidence that Chinese military personnel were also present on the island and possibly helped to develop the Okinawan fighting systems. One such man was named Kushanku. In 1762 an Okinawan ship drifted to Tosa in Japan and a man named Tobe Ryoen was tasked with interviewing and recording the testimony of the passengers and crew. It is said that in his written record, the *Oshima Hikki*, there is reference to Chinese fighting systems on the Okinawan islands and the name of Kusankun is mentioned. The name Kushanku is often referred to in historical documents and it is fair to assume that Kushanku and Kusankun are one and the same. Kusankun was said to have been an expert in Ch'uan fa and had come to Okinawa from China. Kusankun is also said to have trained a man called Shionja from Shuri.

The records relating to Kusankun are unfortunately limited, meaning that to a large degree we have to rely upon word of mouth and folklore.

One account is that Okinawa, feeling threatened by a possible invasion from Japan, requested China to dispatch military officers to advise the king. One of these advisers was Kusankun. The date of this is not clear, although there is an account of a confrontation between Kusankun and the renowned Okinawan master named Sakugawa, who lived between 1733 and 1815. Sakugawa is said to have been a student of Takahara (1683–1760), who is reported to have been a monk and an expert in Shuri-te. After the confrontation with Kusankun, Sakugawa is reported to have received instruction from him with the blessing of Takahara. This, therefore, must have been prior to Takahara's death in 1760.

When Kusankun returned to China, it is said that he was followed by Sakugawa, who trained with him for a further six years. Sakugawa is believed to have been a samurai, which would have made him Japanese and presumably a descendant of the Satsuma clan. In this respect he was also known by the name of Satunuky, or Satonushi.

It is widely believed that the kata Kanku Dai was created or named after Kusankun. One school of thought is that the kata was created by Sakugawa and named after his mentor Kusankun. The connection between Kanku Dai and Kusankun is further evidenced by the kata's older names, which include Kusankun and Kushanku. Kanku Dai is a mainstream Shotokan kata.

Two further Okinawans who are believed to have trained with Kusankun are Bushi Matsumura and Chatan Yara. Bushi Matsumura, a renowned martial artist, is believed to have trained under Sakugawa and is also said to have travelled to China to train under Kusankun directly. While Chatan Yara is said to have trained with Kusankun, the detail is sketchy.

Karate was first introduced to Japan from Okinawa in the early 1900s when Master Gichin Funakoshi travelled to Tokyo and gave two demonstrations of the art. The first was in 1916 and the second in 1922. Following the 1922 demonstration, Kano Jigoro, the famous judo master, approached Funakoshi and asked if he could be taught karate. Funakoshi agreed and began taking his first karate classes at the judo headquarters in Tokyo where Kano and other judoka were his first students. In 1936, Funakoshi established the first purpose-built dojo in Tokyo, which was named the Shotokan and in 1948 the Japan Karate Association (JKA) was founded with Funakoshi as its first Chief Instructor. Over the ensuing years karate spread to virtually every corner of Japan and in time across the globe.

During the first half of the century karate went through a period of intense evolution, with many changes being made by Funakoshi's own admission to make it more acceptable to the Japanese. Karate uniforms and the belt system were introduced, having been copied from judo, which was already systemized. Many of the karate kata had their names changed from the original Okinawan or Chinese names to Japanese. The changes were not just cosmetic – the physical nature of karate also underwent some change. The stances were modified to become much longer, new kicks such as mawashi-geri and keage were added to the system. The kata also had to change to accommodate the different stances and new techniques. It was also during this period that a structured method of kumite training was developed.

This Japanization of karate remains with us today, with karate being almost universally considered to be a traditional Japanese martial art. In reality, however, the development of karate into the martial art we practise today was spearheaded by a few prominent Okinawan martial arts masters 100 years earlier. These men were proficient in the indigenous art of Okinawan 'te' and also studied Chinese fighting systems, often personally training in China or with Chinese masters who visited or lived in Okinawa. The end result was that by the time karate was being introduced into Japan it had become a composite art with a blending of Okinawan and Chinese fighting systems.

3 Vital-Point Striking

For centuries, martial artists have sought to exploit the most vulnerable areas of the human body, to provide the competitive advantage that could make the difference between life and death. Vital-point striking has its foundations in eastern medicine, in particular Chinese acupuncture. We know that acupuncture has been in existence for some 4,500 years, since the time of the Yellow Emperor, Huang Ti (2697–2596BC) and Indian Ayurvedic medicine is even thought to predate this. As the medical systems and theories evolved within India and China, understandably the exponents of unarmed combat, who were developing their systems during the same period, exploited this body of knowledge. As well as developing knowledge of human anatomy and how to heal, the martial artists were also able to identify the most vulnerable areas of the human body to attack, consequently incorporating these 'vital points' within their systems. In fact, many of the martial arts masters of the past not only became very knowledgeable in medical theory, but also in some cases became practising doctors themselves.

Since its discovery, vital-point striking has been constantly developed and has for centuries been an integral part of the fighting systems of the Far East, not only in India and China but also Okinawa, Japan and Korea. Within Indian martial arts, the striking of vital points is referred to as marma-adi, while those having Okinawan or Japanese lineage generally use the term kyusho, meaning 'instant-effect places'. The Chinese use the term dim-mak, meaning 'death touch technique', but also have less commonly used terms for actual vital points: ming tien mo, means 'a fateful spot' and the name tien hsueh translates as 'a vital acupoint'. The Japanese also have other expressions to describe the vital points: etemi, means 'confrontation of the body' and kinsho means 'forbidden places'. The reference to the last provides a link to acupuncture within which there is a list of 'forbidden points' not recommended for use because they were considered too dangerous.

Chang San Feng

It has been suggested that the inventor of vital-point striking was a Chinese man named Chang San Feng, who was knowledgeable regarding acupuncture. Unfortunately, as with many of the historical martial arts stories, the life of Chang San Feng is shrouded in mystery and folklore, although his existence has been generally accepted. He is commonly believed to be the creator of taijiquan, the forerunner of what today is commonly referred to as tai-chi. While nowadays t'ai-chi is, in many instances, taught merely as a form of physical exercise, under closer examination it is, in fact, a very effective system of unarmed combat.

Where and when Chang San Feng lived is not clear. Wong Shiu Han, a leading authority on his legend and life, has calculated that he was born between 1314 and 1320 and died in 1417. Wong Shiu Han states that there was a reference to Chang San Feng's school of martial arts made by Huang Tsung-hsi, a known 'boxer' who from 1610–95. The following is said to have been written by Huang Tsung-hsi: 'In the art of boxing there is the esoteric school which emphasizes the skill of subduing the movement of your opponent by remaining repose, so that your opponent will

Fig. 5   Chang San Feng.

reworked the Shaolin forms to create his own system of taijiquan, incorporating the Taoist philosophy with which he was more aligned.

While reworking the Shaolin forms and developing taijiquan, Chang San Feng is reported to have undertaken significant medical research and begun to include vital points within his system. Patrick McCarthy relates one account in which Chang San Feng is said to have bribed gaolers to allow him to experiment and develop his knowledge of pressure points using prisoners who were awaiting execution. He is also said to have produced a bronze male statue on which over 300 acupuncture points were marked, including the main 108 points used in the martial arts.

Whether or not Chang San Feng was the founder of vital-point striking is the subject of speculation, but it is likely that he had a role in refining the techniques. Interestingly, the existence of vital points was documented before his time. These vital points appeared in 1247 in what is believed to be the oldest book on forensic medicine, called the *Hsi Yuan Lu*, or the *Records of the Washing Away of Unjust Imputations*, more commonly referred to as *Instructions to Coroners*. The document is of particular significance because the author was Sung Tzhu, who for a time was based as a Government official in the Fukien Province on the east coast of China, where we know the early martial arts were flourishing. Sung Tzhu went on to become a judge in Canton. It is believed that the *Hsi Yaun Lu* was developed from other, earlier works, namely the *I Yu Chi* by Ho Ning and the *Nei Shu Lu* by an unknown author. The *Hsi Yuan Lu* refers to thirty-two vital points, shown on two diagrams, and the book advises the owner to mark these points in red.

Most of Okinawa's early contact with China was with the port cities of the Fukien Province, in particular Fuzhou. It is from here that the Chinese community (believed also to have included martial arts experts) known as the thirty-six families settled in Naha, Okinawa, in 1393 (*see* above). This region of China is therefore likely to have been very significant in the transfer of ideas and techniques between the early martial artists.

collapse as soon as you lay hands on him ... This was originated by Chang San Feng'

Legend states that Chang San Feng trained at the Shaolin Temple for ten years and mastered all of the Shaolin forms. It is said that while training there he developed concerns about the hard nature of the martial arts being taught and, as a result, left and went in retreat to a Taoist monastery in the Wudang mountains. There he

The Influence of the *Bubishi*

The most popular and widespread style of martial arts practised in the Fukien Province is White Crane boxing, created by Fang Chi Liang. Fang Chi Liang's father is said to have trained at the southern Shaolin Temple. Significantly, White Crane boxing provides a direct link with the development of vital-point striking, through an ancient manuscript called the *Bubishi*. This is perhaps one of the most important documents on this subject to have come to light in recent years. Often referred to as the 'Bible of karate', the *Bubishi* is a Chinese manuscript containing martial arts history, philosophy and strategy, as well as a section on medicine. It is said that this text was kept and maintained in secret and passed from master to select students only. Two translations of this remarkable text have been made in recent years, both of which are essential reading. The first, published in 1993, was translated by George Alexander and Ken Penland. The second, more comprehensive translation by Patrick McCarthy was published in 1995.

While the author of the *Bubishi* is unknown, the text is most likely to have originated from the White Crane boxing lineage. This is borne out by Article 1 of the manuscript, which provides an insight into the history and philosophy of the White Crane style. Alexander and Penland refer to a theory that the *Bubishi* was a martial arts textbook stemming directly from the southern Shaolin Temple. The *Bubishi* is of great help in sorting out some of the pieces of modern karate's historical jigsaw. Thanks to the substantial research by McCarthy and others, we are able to identify some of the Okinawan masters who either had copies of the *Bubishi* or who were aware of its contents.

From the Naha-te lineage, Kanryo Higaonna is known to have studied Chinese martial arts in the Fukien Province under a Chinese boxing master Liu Liukung. On his return to Okinawa, Kanryo Higaonna reportedly developed the Naha-te style further and from this his disciple Miyagi Chojun created Gojo Ryu. It is within the Gojo Ryu style that the *Bubishi* is considered the 'Bible of karate' and it is thought that Miyagi Chojun was inspired by the 'Eight Poems of the Fist' contained within it when deciding on the name 'Goju', which means hard and soft. The third of the eight poems is translated as 'Everything in the universe is breathing hard [go] and soft [ju], in and out'.

Another Okinawan Naha-te master who studied the *Bubishi* was Nakaima Kenri (1819–79). He is said also to have travelled to China and studied under the same Chinese boxing master; on his return to Okinawa, Nakaima Kenri is believed to have brought back a copy of the *Bubishi*.

There is mention of a Chinese man named Kushankun who is said to have resided for some time in Okinawa and was an adept martial artist. The renowned 'Toudi' Sakugawa is said to have been taught by Kushankun. Sakugawa was a martial arts legend in Okinawa and very influential in the development of Shuri-te. He trained in Fuzhou, Beijing and Satsuma and it is possible

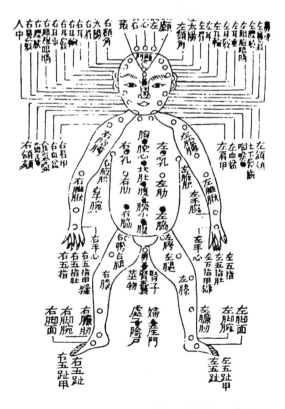

Fig. 6   One of the charts of the *'Hsi Yaun Lu'*.

Fig. 7   Gichin Funakoshi.

that he obtained a copy of the *Bubishi* during his travels.

'Bushi' Matsumura (1797–1889) was an exponent of White Crane boxing and a martial arts instructor to the Okinawan royal family. He is also said to have studied in Fuzhou, Beijing and at the Shaolin Temple. Although there is no direct evidence of his possession of the *Bubishi*, it is considered most likely that he held a copy. He was the creator of Shorin Ryu karate.

There is also the story of a Chinese tea merchant named Gokenki, who arrived in Okinawa from Fukien in the early part of the twentieth century. He is said to have had a copy of the *Bubishi* and used to teach native Okinawans White Crane boxing in the garden at the rear of his teashop. Mubini Kenwa (1889–1953), the founder of Shito Ryu, was one of his students. Mubini Kenwa has referred to his first hand knowledge of a copy of the *Bubishi* being in the possession of Itosu Anko (1832–1915). Itosu taught both Mubini Kenwa and Gichin Funakoshi and, in turn, received instruction himself from 'Bushi' Matsumura from whom it is fair to infer he received his copy of the *Bubishi*. Funa-

koshi made reference to the *Bubishi* in his book *Karate-do Kyohan* (*The Eight Poems of the Fist and Maxims of Sun Tzu*). There are also clear extracts from the *Bubishi* contained within Chapter 6 in the posthumously published book by Funakoshi entitled *Karate Jutsu*. The *Bubishi* was also used by Shimakukuro Tatsuu (1908–75) when establishing Isshin Ryu karate, while the famous Sensei Yamaguchi 'the cat' Gogen (1909–89) referred to it as his most treasured text.

How the Bubishi came to arrive in Okinawa may never be established with any degree of certainty. What is apparent, though, is that it was a significant document to the pioneering Chinese and Okinawan masters. Vital-point striking was a key ingredient of their fighting systems and therefore it follows that any study of the kata, which they created or adapted, would not be complete without an exploration of this fascinating subject. Indeed, the study of vital points is essential to understanding the kata.

Within the following pages some of the more frequently used vital points are identified and many of these will be referred to later on in the bunkai section of this book. A more detailed explanation of the theory and practice of vital-point striking is provided in a previous book by the author, *Secret Karate: The Hidden Pressure Point Techniques of Karate Kata* (The Crowood Press, 2003).

First it is necessary to distinguish between vulnerable areas and pressure points, both of which fall within the term 'vital points'. A vulnerable point is, as its name implies, a part of the body where it is vulnerable and weak, but is not a pressure point. Examples of vulnerable points are the joints, which can be manipulated, bent or even broken to control a person and inflict pain. Another example is the nose, which, being a sensory organ and full of nerves, offers a good striking point and is vulnerable to attack. Pressure points, on the other hand, are different. They can be considered as additional gateways into the body through which pain can be inflicted and the nervous, respiratory and circulatory systems disrupted and even shut down. They are usually identified by their position on acupuncture meridians.

The Lung Meridian Points

LU5: Chize – Cubit Marsh

Located just below the crease of the elbow on the inside of the forearm (Fig. 9).

Note: Strikes to the inside of the forearm in this region are often referred to as LU5, but there are two extra points descending down the forearm from LU5 which are normally the ones used in most applications. These are referred to as M-UE 31 and M-UE 32.

Direction of strike: The direction of strike is into the forearm, with a slight downward angle towards the wrist. The returning hand movement, hikite, found within a number of kata, follows the correct striking pattern for the points.

LU6: Kong Zui – Supreme Hole

Located at the centre of the outside edge (thumb side) of the forearm. This is where the muscle of the forearm connects to the radius (Fig. 9).

Direction of strike: This point should be struck at an angle down along the bone of the arm towards the wrist. When hit correctly, it will send a shock, similar to an electric shock, shooting down the arm.

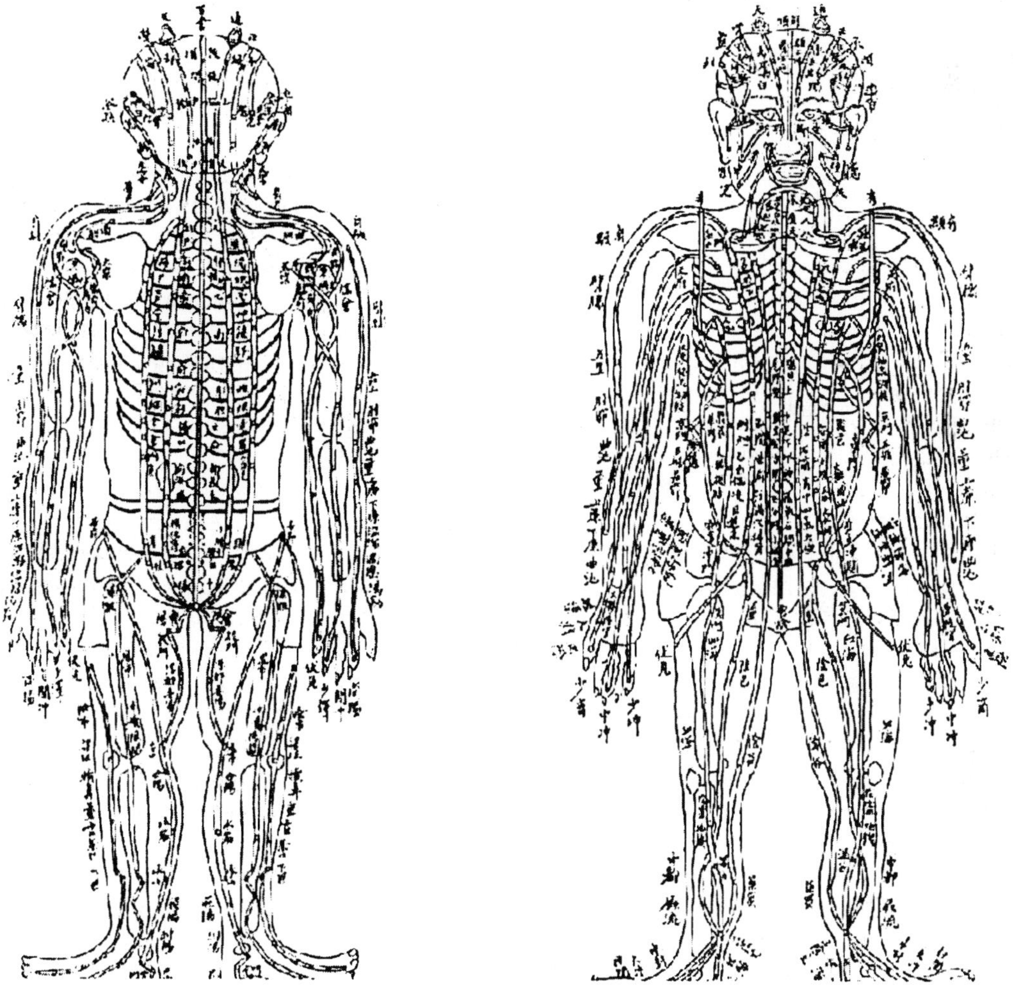

Fig. 8   Old acupuncture charts.

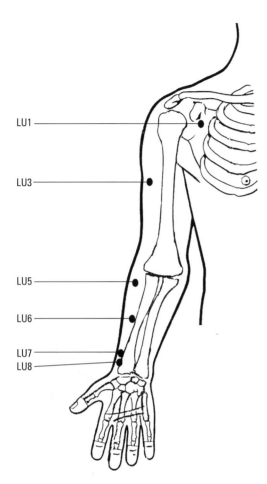

Fig. 9   Points on the lung meridian.

LU7: Lieque – Broken Sequence
Located on the top edge of the radius bone about 1in (2.5cm) from the crease of the wrist (Fig. 9).

Direction of strike: This point should be struck at an angle down, along the bone of the arm towards the wrist. As well as a striking point, LU7 is used in wrist holds. If struck firmly or pressure is applied to it correctly, it will weaken the gripping power of the hand.

LU8: Jingqu – Across the Ditch
Located approximately ¾in (2cm) from the crease of the wrist on the edge of the bone (Fig. 9). (One of the thirty-six points referred to in the *Bubishi*.)

Direction of strike: This point should be struck in the same way as LU7, at an angle down, along the bone of the arm towards the wrist. LU8 is also used in wrist holds. If struck firmly or pressure is applied to it correctly, it will weaken the gripping power of the hand.

The Small Intestine Meridian Points

SI16: Tianchuang – Heaven's Window
Located directly at the centre of the neck in a straight line down from the ear lobe (Fig. 10). (One of the thirty-six points referred to in the *Bubishi*.)

Direction of strike: Straight in from the side towards the centre of the neck. An ideal technique for striking this point is the knife-hand strike (shuto), or the outside of the forearm.

SI18: Quanliao – Cheek Seam
Located just below the cheekbone in a line directly down from the outer edge of the eye (Fig. 10). A very important point from the martial arts perspective and used in many applications.

Direction of strike: This is one of the more dangerous points on the face and care must be

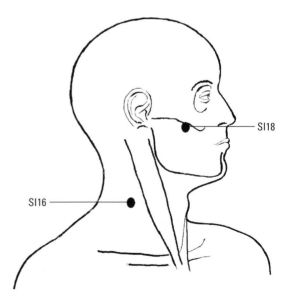

Fig. 10   Small intestine points.

taken when practising here; it is inadvisable to strike this point. The direction of the strike should be in and up towards the centre of the forehead. Pressure can also be applied to this point when a less severe defensive response is required.

The Triple Warmer Meridian Points

TW11: Qinglengyaun – Cooling Gulf

This point is not an effective place to strike, but it responds extremely well to rubbing. It is particularly effective when combined with an arm bar locking technique of the elbow joint. The point is located on the Golgi tendon organ of the triceps muscle (Fig. 11). This is a receptor that is located in the tendons that connect the muscles to the bone. Its primary purpose is to monitor and collect information about the level of tension in the tendon and its associated muscle. By rubbing this point on the arm, the Golgi tendon organ is artificially stimulated, causing the muscle to relax involuntarily, hence its usefulness from the martial arts perspective.

Direction of strike: This point responds to rubbing rather than striking, as noted. Rub directly into the point with a slight downward action towards the wrist to enhance the effect. The rubbing action can be performed with either the fore knuckles or the hard bony part of the back of the wrist.

TW12: Xiaoluo – Melting Luo River

Located directly in the centre of the triceps muscle on the back of the upper arm (Fig. 11).

Direction of strike: Directly inward and in a slightly upward direction. This is an ideal place to attack with a gedan-barai (downward block), which not only activates the point but works against the elbow joint. A hard strike, while simultaneously applying a wrist hold, will cause the attacker to drop to the floor. A consequential effect will be damage to the elbow joint.

TW17: Yifeng – Wind Screen

This point is located in the depression directly behind the ear lobe (Fig. 12). This is probably

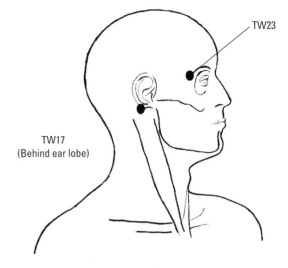

Fig. 11   Triple warmer points.

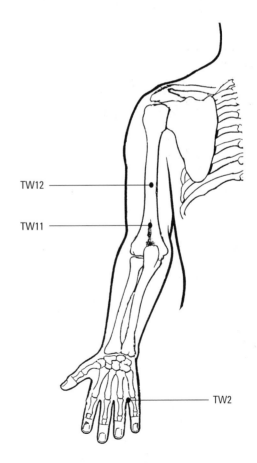

Fig. 12   Triple warmer points.

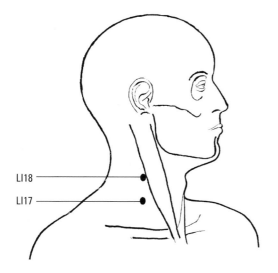

Fig. 13   Large intestine points.

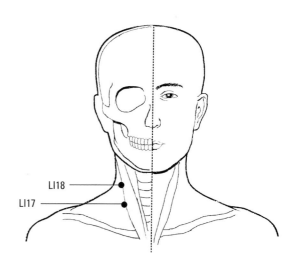

Fig. 14   Large intestine points.

one of the most dangerous pressure points and should never be struck in practice, as brain damage could result. It is one of the vital points mentioned in the *Hsi Yuan Lu* and also one of the thirty-six points referred to in the *Bubishi*. It is a very important point from the martial arts perspective and is used in many applications.

Direction of strike: This point can be struck in two directions: firstly, in an upward direction, in towards the centre of the head; secondly, and more dangerously, from back to front and in slightly.

TW23: Sizhukong – Silken Bamboo Hollow
This is the temple located at either side of the head (Fig. 12).

Direction of strike: Straight in and/or slightly down.

Note: The temple is a very dangerous place to strike.

The Large Intestine Meridian Points

LI17: Tianding – Heaven's Vessel
Located on the front lower neck in a direct line down from the mandible (Figs 13 and 14).

(One of the thirty-six points referred to in the *Bubishi*.)

Direction of strike: This should be struck in a downward direction in towards the centre of the neck. It can also be used by applying pressure as a method of control.

LI18: Futu – Support the Prominence
Located in the centre of the neck in a straight line down and slightly forward from the ear lobe (Figs 13 and 14).

Direction of strike: In a straight line towards the same point on the opposite side of the neck.

The Spleen Meridian Points

SP6: Sanyinjiao – Three Yin Junction
This point is located on the inside of the lower leg approximately 2in (5cm) up from the anklebone (Fig. 15). It is situated in the centre of the leg and over the bone, which means that it is not afforded any muscular protection. This is one of the better targets on the legs because a kick or strike to this area will be painful even without a direct hit on the point. An ideal application is ashi barai (lower leg sweep).

Direction of strike: Directly inward with a slight downward angle.

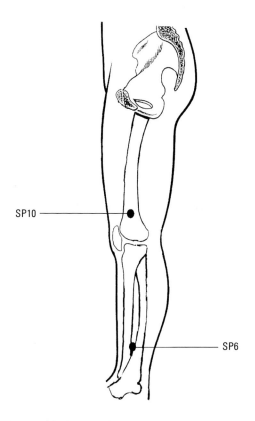

Fig. 15   Spleen points.

SP10: Xuehai

Located just inside the upper leg above the knee (Fig. 15). A strike here will send a shock straight through the body and drop the person to the floor. Kicks using the ball of the foot or heel can be used to good effect here.

Direction of strike: Straight in towards the centre of the leg with an angle slightly to the front.

The Stomach Meridian Points

ST5: Daiying – Big Welcome

Located on the lower edge, approximately at the centre of the jawbone (Fig. 16).

Direction of strike: This point can be struck in either a forward or backward direction along the line of the jawbone. An ideal striking method is using the palm heel (teisho).

ST9: Renying – Man's Welcome

Located at the front of the neck lateral to and level with the thyroid cartilage (Fig. 16). (One of the thirty-six points referred to in the Bubishi.)

Direction of strike: This point can be struck in either a downward or upward direction with either strike penetrating inward slightly at the same time. The most desirable direction of attack to this point will depend upon the comparative height of the attacker and defender. Where the defender is considerably taller than the attacker, it will be more practicable to opt for the downward action and, conversely, the upward direction would be preferable when the attacker is taller.

ST9 is located at a particularly important anatomical location, directly over the carotid sinus, which is a baroreceptor that regulates blood pressure and the flow of blood to the brain. When the carotid sinus detects a change in blood pressure it sends a signal to the brain, via the vagus nerve and the brain responds by altering the blood pressure to stabilize the situation. When this point is struck the process is artificially activated, with the brain being deceived into reacting. The result is that the attacker is knocked out.

Note: Care should be taken when working with this point and it should only be struck in the presence of an experienced instructor.

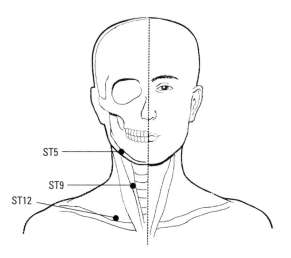

Fig. 16   Stomach points.

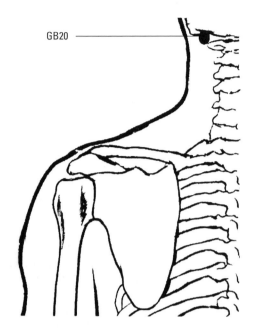

Fig. 17   Gall bladder 20 point.

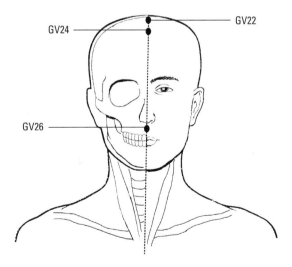

Fig. 18   Governor vessel points.

ST12: Quepen – Empty Basin

Located just behind and at the centre of the clavicle (collar bone) in a line directly up from the nipple (Fig. 16). (One of the thirty-six points referred to in the *Bubishi*.)

Direction of strike: This point is suitable for the applications of pressure. Use the fingers to hook behind the clavicle onto this point. Sawing with the fingers as pressure is applied down can enhance the reaction.

The Gall Bladder Meridian Points

GB20: Fengchih – Pool of Wind

Located at the base of the skull at either side of the top of the spine (Fig. 17). This is a very important point from the martial arts perspective and is used in many applications. It is also key to resuscitation techniques following pressure-point knock-outs.

Direction of strike: The direction of strike is inward and up towards the centre of the head.

The Governor Vessel Meridian Points

GV22: Xinhui – Fontanelle's Meeting

Located at the top and front of the skull (Fig. 18). This is the point on a baby's head that has not closed over at birth. (One of the thirty-six points referred to in the *Bubishi*.)

Direction of strike: Straight down and slightly forward in direction.

GV24: Shenting – Spirit's Hall

Located in the centre and top of the forehead (Fig. 18). (One of the thirty-six points referred to in the *Bubishi*.)

Direction of strike: Straight into the forehead.

GV26: Renzhong – Philtrum

Located directly below the nose in the depression of the upper lip (Fig. 18). (One of the thirty-six points referred to in the *Bubishi*.)

Direction of strike: Straight in and slightly up towards the nose.

Non-Pressure-Point Target Areas

While pressure points are located on acupoints as described above, there are many other vulnerable parts of the body that are not pressure points, but which provide good target areas.

The Temple (Sphenoid Bone)

Being concave in shape, the temple is structurally weak and so a strike to this point should only be undertaken in extreme circumstances. Unconsciousness, brain damage and even death may result. The acupoint TW23 is also located here (*see* above). (One of the thirty-six points referred to in the *Bubishi*.)

Between the Eyes

Between the eyes in the centre of the head is one of the more dangerous striking points. The direction of strike should be in an upward direction, which will cause disorientation, unconsciousness and could prove fatal.

The Eyes

The eyes themselves provide an obvious and good target area. No one likes anything making contact with their eyes, so even the lightest of strikes can produce a good result. The eyes should only be targeted in extreme cases, as blindness, unconsciousness and death could occur. (One of the thirty-six points referred to in the *Bubishi*.)

The Ears

The ears can be used to control an attacker; a strike to the ears with the palm of the hands can result in a perforated eardrum and extreme pain. (One of the thirty-six points referred to in the *Bubishi*.)

The Nose

The nose is full of nerves and bleeds readily, making it a good target area. It is also easily accessible. The lightest of strikes to the nose will cause the eyes to water, resulting in blurred vision or even temporary blindness.

The Neck Area

Irrespective of the presence of a number of pressure points on the neck, the whole of the neck area on both sides provides a good target area but must be selected with care. The jugular vein and carotid artery run along the side of the neck and a blow to this area could rupture or damage either of them, which could result in death.

The Throat

The throat can be divided into two distinct striking areas. Firstly, there is the jugular notch that is located in the centre of the throat below the Adam's apple, but above the manubrium bone (top of the sternum). This is a soft area where the trachea is exposed and unprotected. A slight jab to this point will cause an uncomfortable sensation, while a more powerful strike could prove fatal. The second key area of the throat is the thyroid cartilage. In men, this area is prominent and easily identifiable by the Adam's apple. Even a light strike to this point could prove fatal.

Brachial Plexus

The brachial plexus extends from the lower part of the side of the neck across the shoulders. It marks the union of a number of nerves, thus providing an effective striking point. A good strike to this area will impair the use of the arms.

Xiphoid Process/Solar Plexus

The xiphoid process is a strip of cartilage located at the lower end of the sternum and the solar plexus is situated immediately below it. It is difficult to develop muscle over these areas, making them good gateways into the body. A light strike to this region will wind an attacker, while a powerful blow could result in unconsciousness and damage to the heart.

Side of the Ribs

The side of the ribs is particularly vulnerable to attack because of the lack of muscular protection. It is very easy to wind someone with a light strike to this area; a powerful strike could break the ribs and lead to a punctured Lung.

Kidneys

These are located either side of the back and are partially covered by the last rib. A strike to the kidneys is clearly very dangerous as it could rupture them, causing permanent damage and even death.

Testicles

The testicles provide an obvious striking point on men, although this area is not always accessible.

Coccyx

This is the tailbone, situated at the base of the spine. A strike to this area can cause extreme pain, but it is not always readily accessible.

Knees

The knees are the weak areas of the legs and therefore provide a good target area. It is possible to incapacitate an attacker with a powerful strike to the knees. The direction of attack can be from the front, back or either side.

Shins

The shins provide a good target area because of the lack of muscular protection. The bone is close to the surface here and is vulnerable to attack.

Elbows

A hard strike to the elbow joint, forcing it beyond its normal range of movement, can result in dislocation. Additionally, the elbows provide a good target for applying a locking technique if restraint is the desired outcome.

Wrists

The wrist has a number of pressure points in close proximity. In addition, it can be targeted for locking techniques either alone or in conjunction with the fingers and elbows.

Fingers

Twisting and bending the fingers against the joints' normal range of movement provide a good control technique. With force the fingers can be broken, resulting in extreme pain.

4 What are Kata and the Benefits of Practice?

Kata is a Japanese word that means 'form', which aptly describes what the kata are. They are pre-arranged forms containing sequences of blocks, punches, kicks and strikes delivered from a variety stances in either a forward, backward, side-ward or diagonal direction. They have been arranged into set patterns to provide a means by which offensive and defensive self-defence strategies can be practised, rehearsed and over time perfected. The kata contain strategies for dealing with virtually every conceivable attack scenario, providing different levels of response from locking and restraint through to the application of lethal force, if the situation were to warrant its use. In addition, the kata provide other equally important benefits, such as a vehicle for developing skill in performing the basic karate techniques and, when practised correctly, the kata can offer a well-rounded training regime covering all the elements that contribute to the development and retention of a good level of physical fitness. Importantly, these elements are interrelated. A good level of physical fitness will enable the basic techniques to be performed at an enhanced level, but without good technique and physical fitness the ability to apply self-defence strategies will be weakened. In this chapter, these three aspects of kata practice – physical fitness, development of skill and bunkai (applications) – will be explored in more detail.

Physical Fitness

Physical fitness is a term used to describe the overall physical condition of the body and one often used to describe the ability to perform continuous exercise over an extended period. But when looked at more closely, physical fitness can be broken down into a number of components, each of which can be developed through regular kata training. The main components are as follows:

Agility
The ability to perform a series of explosive power movements to stop and change body direction rapidly. Karate involves constant stops and starts and continually requires fast movement in forward, backward and lateral directions. Good agility is a major asset.

Balance
The ability to control the body's position while either stationary or moving. Good balance and stability provide the base from which to deliver explosive karate techniques with devastating affect. All karate techniques require good balance in order to maximize their effectiveness.

Coordination
The ability to perform complex motor skills. This includes hand–eye coordination to identify and respond to a particular situation and the ability to perform karate techniques while on the move.

Strength
The ability of a muscle or group of muscles to exert force for a short period. Strength is vital to power development and muscular strength also helps to support and protect the body.

Flexibility
The ability to achieve an extended range of movement around a joint. Flexibility is important

to prevent injury and to increase performance by allowing muscles to work over a greater range of movements. Because of the explosive nature of karate and the required range of body movements, good flexibility is essential for maximizing performance.

Power

The ability to exert maximum muscular contraction instantly in an explosive burst of movements. Power consists of a combination of strength and speed and is vital for the delivery of effective karate techniques.

Local Muscular Endurance

This is a single muscle's ability to perform sustained activity or contraction. It is a necessary aspect in the repetition of muscular actions.

Cardiovascular Aerobic Capacity

The ability to exercise for a prolonged period without tiring or needing to rest. The cardiovascular system fulfils many functions, including the transportation of oxygen and nutrients to the liver, the removal of waste products and carbon dioxide and the control of body temperature. Strengthening the cardiovascular system therefore improves the body's overall physiological function, enabling enhanced karate performance.

Reaction Time

The time a person taken to respond to a signal. A good reaction time is absolutely essential in karate, as it enables an opponent's body movements or attacks to be identified early, allowing decisive or evasive action to be taken if necessary.

Speed

The ability to perform a movement quickly. Being able to move quickly between two points provides better opportunity to evade incoming attacks, while also enabling better body positioning for executing techniques.

Once the pattern of a kata has been sufficiently mastered it can be practised at the correct timing. This will include fast, explosive movements in combination with subtler, softer movements and, on occasion, the incorporation of dynamic tension, utilizing a variety of the karate stances. Practising the kata in this way will aid the development of each of the ten elements described above, thus helping to build a greater level of physical fitness and consequently improving performance of the individual karate techniques.

Development of Skill

Regular and focused kata practice will also aid the development of skill in performing the basic karate techniques, which not only include the obvious ability to kick or punch well, but also to do so with proper breathing, correct expansion and contraction of the muscles in coordination with bodily movement and the development of speed, power and mental focus.

The learning and developing of these skills require the relevant movements to be understood and practised in detail until they can be performed smoothly and automatically without conscious thought. The body has to 'learn' what it is being asked to do and to achieve this it has to go through a set physiological sequence. When a new body movement is being taught, the student will at first have to think consciously about each of its components and compel the muscles to move in the required manner. In time, with regular practice, these components will require less and less conscious thought until they become automatic and flow in one continual, smooth movement. So how is this achieved?

The brain is the command centre for all movement. Whether it is a kick, a block, a punch or a simple foot movement, the action will be instigated with an initial thought within the cerebral cortex, which is the part of the brain responsible for conscious thought. The cerebral cortex communicates with the muscles by sending electrical impulses via another part of the brain, the cerebellum. The cerebellum is the muscle-control part of the brain. The nerve impulses commence their onward journey by leaving the brain through the brain stem and enter the spinal cord. The spinal cord has numerous branches attached to it that service all the different areas of the body. These branches are called 'peripheral nerves', which spread around the body like an electrical circuit. The nerve impulses travel from the spinal cord along the peripheral nerves to the relevant muscles whose action is required to generate a specific movement.

In order to learn a new movement it is necessary to establish a neuronal (nervous) pathway for that movement between the brain and the muscles concerned. This is achieved by repeating the same movement hundreds of times. The result is a physical process that causes a structural change at the microscopic level of our neurons. The more times the movement is repeated, the more strongly the neuronal pathway will be established.

Over time, the muscle commands originating in the cerebral cortex are taken over directly by the muscle-control centre of the cerebellum, which in the early learning stage had acted only as a go-between. All that remains at the conscious level is the order to move, for example 'to perform a gedan-barai'. Having received this order the cerebellum will automatically take over and control all the individual movements unconsciously. The end result is that those movements we had concentrate on one by one when we were first learning will have now become instinctive. A simple analogy is learning to drive. At the start, a lot of information has to be taken in, processed and turned into action: check the mirror, depress the clutch, put the car into the right gear, indicate, steer the car in the right direction, brake without stalling and so on. I am sure most people remember the first driving lesson when all this seemed so confusing and difficult. But after a while all these actions will be carried out automatically and the driver is then able to take in his or her surroundings and concentrate on driving the car safely.

Interestingly, and in fact importantly, the process of repeating the movements to achieve this automatic response can be done slowly; the neuronal pathways will still be established. Once these pathways have been sufficiently established, speed and power can then be added. The body will not, however, discriminate between good and bad technique and it will learn whatever movement is being repeated. It is therefore essential that care is taken to practise and repeat only what we want our muscles to learn – that is, the correct technique.

Bunkai (Application) Principles

As already outlined, the kata contain strategies for dealing with virtually every conceivable street self-defence scenario, with an escalating response dependent upon the severity of the threat posed by the attacker. At the lower end of the scale, the defensive response to an attack may allow for restraint involving the use of joint locks or techniques to temporarily incapacitate, while in a life-or-death situation the response could be escalated to the use of lethal force, with strikes to vital points and the exploitation of anatomical weaknesses. Gichin Funakoshi is his book *Karate-do Kyohan*[23] also informs us that there are at least nine throwing techniques used in karate and these should be studied referring to basic kata. If we add to these ground work, sweeps and grappling, then it can be seen that the kata contain a great number of fighting options that are rarely explored and practised within the general karate training regime. In reality, we are often just scratching the surface when exploring kata bunkai.

There are some basic principles that need to be understood when exploring the applications of the moves in kata. It is now almost universally accepted among karate scholars that the defences were designed to be used against a single, untrained assailant; that is, they were not conceived with the martial arts expert attacker in mind, but were directed more at the lay person embarking upon a criminal act and acting alone. They were not created with the intention of fighting multiple opponents. That said, there may be occasions when individual techniques can be employed against multiple assailants, but this was not their initial purpose and the odds will be heavily stacked against the defender. With the untrained non-martial artist in mind, the attacks are generally not going to be straight line attacks or kicks to the upper body and head, but, instead, are more likely to be swinging, circular punches and football-style kicks aimed at the stomach and below. In addition, the attacks will not be delivered from distance in long stances, which is the hallmark of modern karate practice, but from close quarters. Consequently, the kata also contemplate confrontations commencing or moving into a grappling stage.

A further important consideration is how we use techniques described as 'uke' (blocking). Blocks can and often are, used as attacking movements. For example, an age-uke (upper rising block) is not restricted to use against a head punch, but can be used in other ways such as a forearm smash to the face. Gedan-barai (lower-level parrying block) can be used as either a preemptive strike or as a counter-attacking move, in addition to its blocking capabilities.

When exploring the kata with a view to identifying and practising bunkai, it is important not to over-complicate the proposed movements. The aim should be to keep the applications simple so that they can be drilled over and over again until they become instinctive and automatically applied moves capable of being deployed effectively while one is under the stress of being attacked. This is important because the body's in-built defence mechanisms will come into force when under attack, creating physiological responses one has little or no conscious control over. When under attack, the body naturally produces a surge of adrenaline. The results can be quite staggering, especially if you are not used to witnessing, or being, the subject of violence. The mind may become incapable of thinking up complicated offensive or defensive strategies, only the major muscle groups may be capable of being used, hearing may become impaired, peripheral vision may be lost and everything may seem to be in slow motion. It is also possible that the limbs, especially the legs, will start to shake and some people may feel physically sick. It is, however, possible to train the body to react without conscious thought even when confronted with these physiological barriers. The key is to keep the kata bunkai simple and to practise extensively. It is also essential that when training within the dojo as much realism is built into the training regime as is safely possible.

Self-Defence Themes

Patrick McCarthy has undertaken considerable research into kata applications, much of it conducted in Okinawa and China. He has created a list of what he refers to as 'habitual acts of physical violence' (HAPV), which cover the complete range of attacks used commonly in street confrontations (Fig. 19). These thirty-six HAPVs are derived from those identified by generations of the fighting monks of the Shaolin Temple.

Having a knowledge of the HAPVs provides a framework around which kata can be studied and their defensive themes identified. As an example, take HAPV 4, which is a circular punch and a common means of attack employed by an untrained fighter. It can be applied as an attack to the head or to any location on a range from the head down to the stomach, which will include the chest and the side of the ribs. The attacks can be delivered both to the right and left sides of the body, with the attacker's right or left hand. Knowing that this is a frequently used method of attack, it is possible to analyse the moves contained within the kata and to identify those that can be used effectively in defence. The same process can be used to focus on each of the HAPVs. Often the defences identified can be employed against more than one type of attack.

Two-Person Drills

Having identified the attack and its defensive movements, these should be taken out of the kata and practised with a training partner. This aspect of training is essential and is an integral part of kata practice. It is through such practice that the techniques and your abilities can be pressure-tested. In the initial stages the attacks and defences should be practised slowly to develop the ability to work the routines with the correct technique. It is absolutely vital, though, that as ability and confidence improve, the speed of delivery is increased until full speed is reached in both attack and defence. The aim of practice in the dojo must be to replicate closely a real situation but in a safe way. As Master Itosu wrote:

'Karate should be practised with intensity, as if you are on the battlefield.'[24] Partner work also plays an essential role in developing faster reaction time.

Visualization

In addition to practising the kata movements as two-person drills the kata should be regularly performed without a partner while also visualizing the defensive application of each move. In reality, this means practising the kata in the sequence as taught and as though you actually had an opponent. As each movement is performed think about applying the moves practised as two-person drills. The advantage of practising the kata without a partner in this way is that full speed and power can be used and the individual techniques can be worked on so as to improve all-round performance. Through visualization, the two-person drills and the solo performance of the kata complement one another.

Without visualization, the kata revert solely to a form of physical exercise and the fundamental martial aspect is lost. The importance of visualization has been passed down to us by the past masters. Master Itosu wrote, 'Karate kata should be practised with its practical use in your mind.'[25] Gichin Funakoshi wrote, 'Your opponent must always be present in your mind,'[26] and that 'knowledge of just the sequence of a form in karate is useless.'[27]

1	straight kicks	20	front under-arm bear hug (and side variation)
2	angular-type kicks	21	front/rear tackle
3	straight punches	22	one-handed wrist grab (same and opposite sides-normal/reversed)
4	circular punches	23	two-handed wrist grabs (normal/reversed)
5	downward strikes	24	both wrists seized from the front/rear
6	upward strikes	25	both arms seized from the front/rear
7	knee and elbow strikes	26	single/double shoulder grab from front/rear
8	head-butt/biting and spitting	27	arm-lock (behind the back)
9	testicle squeeze	28	front arm-bar (triceps tendon fulcrum up supported by wrist)
10	augmented foot/leg trips	29	side arm-bar (triceps tendon fulcrum down supported by wrist)
11	single/double-hand hair pull from the front/rear	30	single/double lapel grab
12	single/double-hand choke from the front/rear	31	single/double-hand shove
13	front neck choke from rear	32	garment pulled over the head
14	classical head-lock	33	seized and impact
15	front, bent-over, augmented choke (neck-hold)	34	single/double leg/ankle grab from the front (side/rear)
16	half/full-nelson	35	ground straddle
17	rear over-arm bear hug (and side variation)	36	attacked (kicked/struck) while down
18	rear under-arm bear hug (and side variation)		
19	front over-arm bear hug (and side variation)		

Fig. 19 Patrick McCarthy's Habitual Acts of Physical Violence.

5 The Kata

Traditionally, the first six karate kata to be taught are Taikyoku Shodan and the five Heian kata, Shodan through to Godan. These six kata are covered in the author's earlier book, *Shotokan Karate – Unravelling the Kata* (The Crowood Press, 2006). When combined, the kata incorporate the majority of the basic karate blocks, punches and stances and provide a good foundation from which to graduate to the intermediate and advanced kata covered in this book, taking the student up to Shodan (first-degree Black Belt level). After Heian Godan, it is usual for the kata Tekki Shodan to be taught, followed by Bassai Dai. These are used for gradings up to 2nd Kyu. For 1st Kyu and Shodan, the kata are usually taken from Ji'in, Jion, Jitte, Kanku Dai or Enpi.

Taikyoku Shodan

There are three Taikyoku kata, of which Shodan is the main one practised today. Some styles refer to this kata as Kihon, meaning basic kata ,which is the original intention of the Taikyoku kata. They were created by Master Funakoshi and his son Yoshitaka to assist beginners with practising basic techniques. The term Taikyoku means 'first cause'.

The Heian Kata

The Heian kata are now firmly established as the backbone of most traditional karate styles from the Shuri-te lineage and feature as the grading kata in most associations for grades up to 4th Kyu. The name Heian means 'peaceful mind' and comes from a merging of the Japanese words heiwa and antei, meaning peace and stability.

Gichin Funakoshi wrote that having mastered the five Heian forms, a man can be confident that he is able to defend himself competently in most situations and that the meaning of the name is to be taken in this context.[28]

The original Okinawan name for the kata was Pinan but was changed by Gichin Funakoshi to Heian in order to make them more palatable to the Japanese. This move was, however, controversial and not universally adopted. Shoshin Nagamine specifically states that the kata should be called Pinan and not Heian,[29] and Pinan is how the kata are referred to in many styles today.

The Japanese characters for Heian are 平安. These same two characters in Chinese translate to ping'an, from which the name Pinan is clearly derived. The Chinese word ping 平 means peaceful, calm and balanced and an 安 means peaceful, secure and content, so when the two characters are combined ping'an means to be peaceful.

It is almost universally accepted that the Pinan kata were developed by Master Itosu between 1901 and 1907 and were originally intended for inclusion in the karate curriculum of the Okinawan school system. Itosu was one of the first Okinawan masters to lift the veil of secrecy that surrounded karate and began to teach it publicly at the turn of the twentieth century. In 1901, Itsou was successful in introducing karate into the Okinawan school physical education curriculum and taught at the Shuri Jinjo elementary school. He later went on to teach at the Shuri Dai-ichi Middle School and the Okinawa Prefectural Men's Normal school in 1905. It is said that he devised the Pinan kata to include basic blocking and punching techniques to make it easier for the pupils to learn. Before then, the first kata traditionally taught was the Naihanchi (Tekki) kata, which is quite intricate and complex in comparison.

From where Itosu obtained his inspiration for the kata is unclear. There is one theory that he in fact reworked earlier Chinese forms known as Channan, but this cannot be corroborated. The name Channan is, however, often referred to in the context of these kata. One theory refers to Channan being a Chinese sailor who was shipwrecked and living in a cave in Tomari. Itosu is said to have befriended him and learnt a kata from him. This kata has been variously referred to as Chiang Nan or Channan. But irrespective of its name, Itosu is said to have simplified the kata he had been taught by breaking it up into five forms, which became the Pinan and Heian kata as we know them today. A further theory is that Itosu created the kata by taking moves from the more advanced karate kata. This certainly makes sense because all the moves contained within the Heian kata can be found spread amongst the more advanced kata, in particular the Kanku and Bassai kata.

Tekki Shodan

Prior to the creation of the Taikyoku and Heian kata, the Tekki kata was the first to be taught. Its original Okinawan name was Naihanchi, which is how it is still referred to in some schools today. The change of name to the Japanese Tekki was made by Master Gichin Funakoshi in order to make it more palatable to the Japanese when exporting karate from Okinawa. Naihanchi means 'horse-riding' and its name derives from the extensive use within the kata of kiba-dachi (horse-riding stance). There are currently three Tekki kata: Shodan, Nidan and Sandan. It is, however, thought that the original Naihanchi kata was a single but long kata comprising moves from all three modern forms. The division of the kata into three was made by Master Ankoh Itosu in order to make it easier to learn. Naihanchi was Master Itosu's favourite kata and he taught it to Master Funakoshi over a three-year period. It is believed that Master Itosu learned the kata from 'Bushi' Matsumura.

Bassai Dai

The word Bassai means 'to penetrate a fortress' and it is a strong, powerful kata. Its movements are said to be reminiscent of a battering ram being used against solid walls. The kata originates from either the Tomari-te or Shuri-te lineage and was another popular kata with Master Itosu. The Bassai kata comes in two forms, the original Bassai Dai (Dai meaning big) and a second kata Bassai Sho (Sho meaning small) created by master Itosu.

Ji'in

Ji'in, Jion and Jitte all commence from the same specific yoi (ready) position which is a Chinese salutation, thus signifying their Chinese origins. One theory is that the kata originate from the Jion Temple in China where the monks were ardent martial artists, although there is no real evidence to back this up.

Ji'in means 'love and shadow' and is believed to have been developed through the Tomari-te lineage. It was originally called Shokyo by Gichin Funakoshi and is not one that he practised or taught extensively.

Jion

Jion is the kata's original name and it is one of the most long-established kata of the Shotokan style. Its name translates as 'love and goodness' and it has clear Chinese origins, commencing and ending with a traditional Chinese salutation.

Jitte

Jitte's original name was Jutte, meaning 'ten hands': ju means 'ten' and te 'hands'. It is claimed that this kata helps to prepare the student to defend against ten opponents, although this is rather fanciful. Another theory says that the name derived from the Jitte, a traditional Okinawan martial arts weapon. As with Ji'in, the kata is thought to have come from the Tomari-te school.

Kanku Dai

Kanku means 'to view the sky' and its name derives from the opening move. The kata was one of Master Funakoshi's favourites and is a cornerstone of the Shotokan style. It is widely believed that this kata was created or named after the Chinese master, Kusankun. One school of thought is that the kata was created by Sakugawa and named after his mentor Kusankun. The connection between Kanku Dai and Kusankun is further evidenced by the kata's older names, which include Kusankun and Kushanku.

The Kanku kata comes in two forms, the original Kanku Dai (Dai meaning big) and a second kata Kanku Sho (Sho meaning small) created by Master Itosu.

Enpi

Enpi (sometimes referred to as Empi) was originally named Wanshu and means 'flight of the swallow', which is derived from the fast dipping and rising techniques contained within it. The kata originated through the Tomari-te lineage although its exact origins are lost in antiquity.

The Stages of Learning the Kata

There are many academic behaviourist theories on how we learn a new skill, but perhaps the most pertinent to karate and the kata is one suggested by two American psychologists, P.M. Fitts and M.I. Posner, in their 1967 book, *Human Performance*. They state that the learning process is sequential and that we move through three specific phases as we learn:

Cognitive phase: During this stage, the learner is seeking to understand what they have to do and how they will achieve it. It involves the identification and development of the component parts of the skill.

Associative phase: The learner will enter this phase once a basic understanding of the component parts that make up the skill has been acquired. Time will then be spent on practising and refining the skill, reducing and eliminating errors.

Autonomous phase: This phase is reached when the learner has developed the skill so that it becomes automatic, involving little or no conscious thought.

Relating these phases of kata, the training process becomes more logical. In seeking to learn a new kata it is necessary to go through three stages of learning similar to the Fitts and Posner model.

Stage One

The first (cognitive) stage is to learn the basic techniques and the kata's pattern. For the beginner or a student in the early years of training, this stage can prove to be challenging. Not only is there the requirement to memorize the new pattern, but also the brain still having to think consciously about the mechanics of each individual move. The analogy is with learning to drive, as noted earlier.

It is always worth remembering that the individual techniques are often not complex and can be taken out of the kata and practised in isolation. It is putting the techniques together in the required sequence that often presents difficulty and confusion, making the kata appear more complex than they in fact are. Time needs to be taken at this first stage so that the techniques are performed in the correct stances and at the correct angles. Almost all karate kata start and finish at the same point on the floor. When this fails to happen it is often inconsistent stances or wrong angles that are the cause.

For the more experienced karate student, the process of learning a new kata can be less daunting because a reasonable level of skill in the individual techniques that make up the kata has already been acquired; the brain therefore has less information to process and the main focus of stage one can be on learning the pattern.

Stage Two

Having learnt the basic techniques and the pattern of the kata, the second stage of learning (the associative phase) involves perfecting the individual techniques ensuring that everything falls into place at the right time – that is, correct technique, fluidity of movement, proper breathing, correct stance, mental focus, speed of movement and all the elements that go to make karate such an explosive and dynamic martial art. This second stage of learning can take many years of training before anywhere near perfection is achieved.

Stage Three

The third, autonomous, stage of learning requires an understanding of the purpose of each movement – that is, its intended application against one of the myriad of attack scenarios or acts of physical violence and then to perform the kata with perfect technique while visualizing the attack or defence being employed for each move. It is during this stage that the movements become automatic, reactive responses capable of being performed without conscious thought. Much of the work at stage one and two will be a case of helping to develop the ability to move automatically in this way. Training in stage three will be continuing this development by refining and using the techniques in confrontation situations.

It is not necessary to complete the whole of the kata at stage one before graduating to stage two and later to stage three. All three stages of learning can be employed at the same time from the start. For example, if one were to take the first move of Heian Shodan, which is a gedan-barai (downward block), it is possible to learn this block, understand, seek to perfect it and practise it against an incoming punch to the stomach, all within a short period. The ultimate aim is, however, to perform the whole kata at stage three. It is then that the kata will come to life, with the physical and non-physical elements uniting into a powerful and effective martial arts routine.

Stage one, while sometimes difficult, is pretty much self-explanatory and can be achieved by everyone with perseverance. Unfortunately, it is rare for anyone to attain successfully a perfected stage two and even rarer for someone to start seriously to achieve stage three for a complete kata. In respect of stage two, this is often due to a lack of understanding of the physiological and psychological processes involved, while stage three often proves elusive because of a lack of available knowledge and instruction.

The Kata

In the following pages the kata are demonstrated and their movements explained. The format for each kata is the same, each one being broken down step by step through a series of photographs. These photographs are all taken from the same camera position, which is directly in front at the commencement of the kata. Where the photographs show a rear view or a view that is difficult to see, additional photographs are provided separately at the end to help with understanding. A descriptive account of each movement of the kata is also provided to explain the finer detail. This approach of combining photographs and descriptive account provides a unique and invaluable learning aid.

Kata Directional Aid

To assist with identifying the direction of some of the less obvious movements, the compass figure (Fig. 20) can be used as a point of reference.

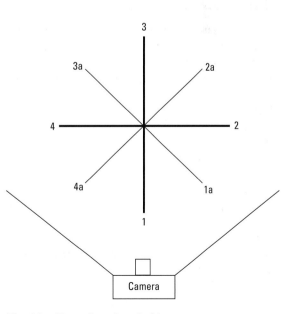

Fig. 20   Kata directional aid.

6 Tekki Shodan

The Kata

Step 1: Rei (bow)
Commence the kata with a bow (Figs 21 and 22). This can be in either musubi-dachi or heisoku-dachi. The choice of stance varies between Associations.

Step 2: Yoi (ready position)
After the bow step out with the right foot into heiko-dachi (parallel stance) and the usual yoi position (Fig. 23).

Step 3: Tekki yoi (specific Tekki ready position)
The next movement is a step into the specific Tekki yoi (Tekki ready) position. To achieve this move the right foot to the left into a heisoku-dachi (informal attention stance), while at the same time bringing the hands together so that the left hand covers the right (Fig. 24). The hands must be positioned at groin height.

Note: The movement of the right foot and hands must take place at the same time.

Step 4: Kosa-dachi (crossed-legged stance)
Commence the movement by turning the head to the right and then immediately step over with the left foot into kosa-dachi (crossed-legged stance) (Fig. 25). The left foot should be touching the ground with the ball of the foot only.

Fig. 21 Musubi-dachi.

Fig. 22 Rei.

Fig. 23 Yoi.

Fig. 24 Tekki yoi.

Fig. 25   Kosa-dachi.

Fig. 26   Intermediate stage.

Fig. 27   Side view.

Fig. 28   Fumikomi/haishu-uke.

Fig. 29   Empi-uchi.

Fig. 30   Hikite.

Step 5: Fumikomi/haishu-uke (stamping kick/back hand block)

The next movement is a fumikomi (stamping kick) with the right foot, while at the same time blocking with the right hand. Commence by raising the right knee, while at the same time crossing the arms at the front; keep the head facing right (Fig. 26). This is the intermediate stage.

Note: The foot does not extend far beyond the knee in this technique (Fig. 27), although some schools teach this as a mikazuki-geri (crescent kick).

From this position, stamp down with the right foot into a kiba-dachi (horse-riding stance) and strike out with the right hand so that the arm completes locked straight with the back of the hand facing to the rear (Fig. 28).

In application this can be either a block or strike, using either the back of the hand or in some cases the back of the arm.

Step 6: Empi-uchi (elbow strike)

Remaining in kiba-dachi (horse-riding stance), pull the right hand back and strike the palm of the

Fig. 31   Gedan-barai.

Fig. 32   Kage-zuki.

Fig. 33   Kosa-dachi.

Fig. 34   Intermediate stage.

Fig. 35   Fumikomi/uchi-uke.

Fig. 36   Intermediate stage.

hand with the left elbow, performing a mawashi-empi-uchi (roundhouse elbow strike) (Fig. 29). The head remains facing the right at this stage.

Step 7: Hikite (pulling hands)

Again maintaining the same kiba-dachi (horse-riding stance) position, move both hands to the right hip as fists into the hikite (pulling hands) position (Fig. 30). During this movement, the head must turn sharply left.

Step 8: Gedan-barai/kage-zuki (lower-level block/hook punch)

Without changing the stance or head position, perform a single-handed gedan-barai (lower-level block) with the left hand (Fig. 31). Immediately follow with a right kage-zuki (hook punch) (Fig. 32).

Note: The fist of the right hand should complete the movement level with the left hip so that the fist does not extend beyond the hip and the forearm must end at a slight downward angle.

Step 9: Kosa-dachi (crossed-legged stance)

Step to the left with the right foot so that it

Fig. 37   Intermediate stage.

Fig. 38   Ura-zuki/kage-zuki.

Fig. 39   Nami-ashi.

Fig. 40
Gaiwan-uke.

crosses the left foot into kosa-dachi (crossed-legged stance) without changing the head or hand positions (Fig. 33). The left foot should be flat on the ground and the right positioned so that the side of the foot only is in contact with the ground.

Step 10: Fumikomi/uchi-uke (stamping kick/inside forearm block)

Commence this move by raising the left knee in preparation for the fumikomi (stamping kick), while at the same time turning the head to the front and pulling the right hand back to the chest (Fig. 34). This is the intermediate stage. It is important to ensure that the left foot does not

extend too far in front of the knee at this point. Continue by stamping down with the left foot, completing in kiba-dachi (horse-riding stance) and simultaneously blocking uchi-uke (inside forearm block) with the right hand (Fig. 35).

Step 11: Gedan-barai/haiwan-uke (lower-level block/back arm block)

Commence this movement by crossing the arms in front of the body with the left arm in front (Fig. 36). From this position, punch out to the front in a slight downward direction with the right fist, while at the same time pulling the left arm back above shoulder height (Fig. 37). The head remains facing forward.

Step 12: Ura-zuki/kage-zuki (upper cut punch/hook punch)

Move the left hand down and then up and out to perform the ura-zuki (upper cut punch), so that in the final part of the movement the fist is punching upwards. At the same time, the right hand should be drawn back to the kage-zuki (hook punch) position with the elbow of the left arm making contact with the back of the right fist (Fig. 38).

Step 13: Nami-ashi/gaiwan-uke (pulling up leg/outer forearm block)

The sequence for the next two movements is a

41

Fig. 41   Nami-ashi.

Fig. 42   Soto-ude-uke.

Fig. 43   Hikite.

Fig. 44   Morote-zuki.

Fig. 45   Intermediate stage.

Fig. 46   Haishu-uke.

head turn, followed by the nami-ashi and then the block. Commence by turning the head sharply left. Then without moving the head or hands perform a nami-ashi (pulling up leg) kick with the left foot, making sure the hips do not rise (Fig. 39). Return the left foot to the kiba-dachi (horse-riding stance) position and simultaneously block with the left forearm, rotating the lower arm by pivoting at the elbow (Fig. 40).

Step 14: Nami-ashi/soto-ude-uke (pulling up leg/outer forearm block)

The sequence for the next two movements is a head turn, followed by the nami-ashi and then

the block. Commence by turning the head sharply right. Then without moving the head or hands perform a nami-ashi (pulling up leg) kick with the right foot, making sure the hips do not rise (Fig. 41). Return the right foot to the kiba-dachi (horse-riding stance) position and simultaneously block soto-ude-uke (outside forearm block) with the left forearm, rotating the lower arm by pivoting at the elbow (Fig. 42).

Step 15: Hikite/morote-zuki (pulling hands/augmented punch)

Without changing the stance, drop the hands to the right hip into the hikite (pulling hands) posi-

Fig. 47   Empi-uchi.

Fig. 48   Hikite.

Fig. 49   Gedan-barai.

tion, while turning the head sharply left (Fig. 43). Immediately follow this by thrusting both fists out to the left to perform the morote-zuki (augmented punch) and kiai (Fig. 44).

Note: The left hand is lower than the right but both are locked straight.

Step 16: Haishu-uke (back of hand block)
Without changing the stance or the head position, cross the arms at the front, keeping the hands as fists with the backs of the hands facing up (Fig. 45). This is the intermediate stage. Then slowly and with dynamic tension move the left arm out to the left and pull the right fist back to the right hip (Fig. 46). As the left hand moves to the left, the hand should slowly open and the lower arm rotate at the elbow so that the arm is straight at the completion of the movement, with the back of the hand facing to the rear.

Step 17: Empi-uchi (elbow strike)
Remaining in kiba-dachi (horse-riding stance), pull the left hand back and strike the palm of the hand with the right elbow, performing a mawashi-empi-uchi (roundhouse elbow strike) (Fig. 47). The head remains facing the left at this stage.

Step 18: Hikite (pulling hands)
Maintaining the kiba-dachi (horse-riding stance)

position, move both hands to the left hip as fists into the hikite (pulling hands) position (Fig.48). During this movement the head must turn sharply right.

Step 19: Gedan-barai/kage-zuki (lower-level block/hook punch)
Without changing the stance or head position, perform a single-handed gedan-barai (lower-level block) with the right hand (Fig. 49). Immediately follow with a left kage-zuki (hook punch) (Fig. 50).

Note: The fist of the left hand should complete the movement level with the right hip so that the fist does not extend beyond the hip.

Fig. 50   Kage-zuki.

Fig. 51   Kosa-dachi.

Fig. 52   Intermediate stage.

Fig. 53   Fumikomi/uchi-uke.

Fig. 54   Intermediate stage.

Fig. 55   Intermediate stage.

Fig. 56   Ura-zuki/kage-zuki.

Step 20: Kosa-dachi (crossed-legged stance)

Step to the right with the left foot so that it crosses the right foot into kosa-dachi (crossed-legged stance) without changing the head or hand positions (Fig. 51). The right foot should be flat on the ground and the left positioned so that the side of the foot only is in contact with the ground.

Step 21: Fumikomi/uchi-uke (stamping kick/inside forearm block)

Commence this move by raising the right knee in preparation for the fumikomi (stamping kick), while at the same time turning the head to the front and pulling the left hand back to the chest (Fig. 52). This is the intermediate stage. It is important to ensure that the right foot does not extend too far in front of the knee at this point. Continue by stamping down with the right foot, completing in kiba-dachi (horse-riding stance) and simultaneously blocking uchi-uke (inside forearm block) with the left hand (Fig. 53).

Fig. 57   Nami-ashi.

Fig. 58   Gaiwan-uke.

Fig. 59   Nami-ashi.

Step 22: Gedan-barai/haiwan-uke (lower-level block/back arm block)

Commence this movement by crossing the arms in front of the body with the right arm in front (Fig. 54). From this position, punch out to the front in a slight downward direction with the left fist, while at the same time pulling the right arm back above shoulder height (Fig. 55). The head remains facing forward.

Step 23: Ura-zuki/kage-zuki (upper cut punch/hook punch)

Move the right hand down and then up and out to perform the ura-zuki (upper cut punch), so that in the final part of the movement the fist is punching upwards. At the same time, the left hand should be drawn back to the kage-zuki (hook punch) position, with the elbow of the right arm making contact with the back of the left fist (Fig. 56).

Step 24: Nami-ashi/gaiwan-uke (pulling up leg/outer forearm block)

The sequence for the next two movements is a head turn followed by the nami-ashi and then the block. Commence by turning the head sharply right. Then without moving the head or hands perform a nami-ashi (pulling up leg) kick with the right foot, making sure the hips do not rise (Fig. 57). Return the right foot to the kiba-dachi

Fig. 60   Soto-ude-uke.

(horse-riding stance) position and simultaneously block with the right forearm, rotating the lower arm by pivoting at the elbow (Fig. 58).

Step 25: Nami-ashi/soto-ude-uke (pulling up leg/outside forearm block)

The sequence for the next two movements is a head turn followed by the nami-ashi and then the block. Commence by turning the head sharply left. Then without moving the head or hands perform a nami-ashi (pulling up leg) kick with the left foot, making sure the hips do not rise (Fig. 59). Return the left foot to the kiba-dachi (horse-riding stance) position and simultaneously block soto-ude-uke (outside forearm block) with the right forearm, rotating the lower arm by pivoting at the elbow (Fig. 60).

45

Fig. 61   Hikite.

Fig. 62   Morote-zuki.

Fig. 63   Intermediate stage.

Fig. 64   Yame.

Fig. 65   Yoi.

Fig. 66   Rei.

Step 26: Hikite/morote-zuki (pulling hands/augmented punch)

Without changing the stance, drop the hands to the left hip into the hikite (pulling hands) position, while turning the head sharply right (Fig. 61). Immediately follow this by thrusting both fists out to the right to perform the morote-zuki (augmented punch) and kiai (Fig. 62).

Step 27: Yame (finish position)

The next move is a return to the kata yoi (ready) position. To do this move the right foot into the left so that the feet end in heisoku-dachi (infor-mal attention stance). At the same time, move the hands back to the centre of the body so that the left hand ends up on top of the right (Figs 63 and 64). This is a slow movement. From this position, move the right foot out into heiko-dachi (parallel stance) and cross the arms in front of the body, returning to the conventional ready position (Fig. 65).

Step 28: Rei (bow)

To complete the kata, step with the right foot back into heisoku-dachi and perform a finishing bow (Fig. 66).

Fig. 67   Wrist grab.

Fig. 68   Rotation of wrist.

Fig. 69   Haishu-uke.

Fig. 70   Strike to back of head.

Fig. 71   Elbow strike.

Selected Bunkai

Steps 5 and 6: Haishu-uke/empi-uchi

The opening moves of the kata have a variety of different applications. In the example provided here the move is used to defend against a wrist grab in which the attacker grabs the defender's right wrist with the left hand.

To defend, commence by opening the hand, which expands the muscles of the wrist, and rotate the hand clockwise (Figs 67 and 68).

From this position, thrust the right arm out in a straight line as in the kata (Fig. 69). In most cases this will result in the wrist being released. Follow up immediately with a counter-attack by striking the back of the head with the right palm and striking the face with an elbow strike (Figs 70 and 71).

The palm-heel strike to the back of the head can be used to strike the pressure point GB20, which, if hit with sufficient force, may result in a knock-out.

47

Fig. 72   Take-down by rotating the neck.

Fig. 73   Simultaneous block and strike.

Fig. 74   Lapel grab.

Fig. 75   Strike into crease of elbow.

Fig. 76   Ura-zuki.

Steps 6 and 7: Empi-uchi/hikite

The movement from the empi-uchi (elbow strike) to the hikite (pulling hands) position can be used as a take-down technique. To achieve this after the elbow strike maintain tight contact with the head between the right hand and the forearm and rotate the head around and in a downward angle. This will enable the attacker to be kept under control and taken down to the ground (Fig. 72). If this movement is performed quickly it may result in neck damage.

Step 11: Gedan-barai/haiwan uke

The gedan-barai (lower-level block) and haiwan-uke (back arm block) can be used as a simultaneous block and counter-attack against a punch to

Fig. 77   Two-handed grab.

Fig. 78   Nami-ashi.

Fig. 79   Take-down.

the head. In this application the gedan-barai is used to punch in a downward direction and the right arm used to block the punch (Fig. 73).

Step 12: Ura zuki/kage-zuki

In this application the defence is against a right lapel grab in preparation for a punch (Fig. 74). Use the kage-zuki movement to strike downward into the crease of the elbow of the attacker's grabbing left arm (Fig. 75). Hit hard enough and the attacker's legs will buckle and head drop down. To complete the movement, punch with the ura-zuki into the attacker's face (Fig. 76).

Steps 13 and 14: Nami-ashi/gaiwan-uke/soto-ude-uke

The foot movement nami-ashi (pulling up leg) can be used as a kick to the shin, knee or to the vital point Spleen 6 just above the knee. In this first application it is demonstrated as a take-down technique against someone who is grabbing hold with both arms.

Use the nami-ashi kicking action to kick out the attacker's front leg, while at the same time twisting the attacker's body to the right so that balance is lost (Figs 77–79).

An alternative application is to use the ashi-barai as an off-balancing or sweeping technique, following up with a strike to the head using the gaiwan-uke (Fig. 80). The target area for the strike could be the pressure point Triple Warmer 17 behind the ear, or Gall Bladder 20 at the back of the head.

Fig. 80   Nami-ashi/gaiwan-uke.

49

7 Bassai Dai

The Kata

Step 1: Yoi (ready position)

Start the kata with a bow (Figs 81 and 82). After the bow, step out with the right foot into heiko-dachi (parallel stance) and the yoi position (Fig. 83). The next movement is a step into the specific Bassai yoi position. To achieve this, move the right foot to the left into a heisoku-dachi (informal attention stance), while at the same time bringing the hands together so that the left hand encircles the right (Fig. 84). The hands must be positioned at groin height with the arms slightly bent at the elbows.

Step 2: Hiza-geri/migi uchi-uke (knee kick/right inside forearm block)

Raise the right knee at a 45-degree angle, while at

Fig. 81 Musubi-dachi.

Fig. 82　Rei.

Fig. 83　Yoi.

Fig. 84　Bassai Dai yoi.

50

Fig. 85   Hiza-geri.

Fig. 86   Migi uchi-uke.

Fig. 87   Hidari uchi-uke.

Fig. 88   Kosa-dachi/migi uchi-uke.

Fig. 89   Intermediate stage.

Fig. 90   Hidari uchi-uke.

the same time pulling the arms across and behind the body, keeping the hands clasped together as at the yoi position in step 1 (Fig. 85). To continue the movement take a big step forward with the right foot and as the foot lands slide the left foot up behind the right into kosa-dachi (crossed-legged stance) and perform the uchi-uke (inside forearm block) (Fig. 86).

Note: At the end of this movement the left hand should be open and positioned at the inside of the right forearm.

Step 3: Hidari uchi-uke (left inside forearm block)

Step back hip width into a left zenkutsu-dachi (front stance), while at the same time performing a left inside forearm block (Figs 87–90) in direction 3 (Fig. 20). Ensure at the end of the movement that the feet are hip-width apart and the hips sideways on.

51

Fig. 91   Gyaku uchi-uke.

Fig. 92   Gyaku uchi-uke.

Fig. 93   Migi gaiwan-uke.

Fig. 94   Gyaku soto-ude-uke.

Fig. 95   Migi uchi-uke.

Fig. 96   Sukui-uke.

Step 4: Gyaku uchi-uke (reverse inside forearm block)

The stance remains left zenkutsu-dachi (front stance) during this move, although the hips turn to end square to the front and the front foot is pulled back slightly. Commence by crossing the right arm across the front of the body, while pushing the left hand forward and then continue the movement to complete the right gyaku uchi-uke (reverse inside forearm block), pulling the left hand back to the hip (Figs 91 and 92).

Step 5: Migi gaiwan-uke/hidari gyaku soto-ude-uke (right forearm block/left reverse outside forearm block)

Move the rear foot across twice hip width in preparation for the turn, while at the same time rotating the hips so that the right arm moves to the right performing the gaiwan-uke (forearm block) (Fig. 93). Continue with the turn so that the move completes in a right zenkutsu-dachi (front stance), while at the same time performing a left gyaku soto-ude-uke (reverse inside

Fig. 97   Intermediate stage.

Fig. 98   Migi soto-ude-uke.

Fig. 99   Gyaku uchi-uke.

forearm block) (Fig. 94). The right hand returns to the hip.

Step 6: Migi uchi-uke (right inside forearm block)

Without changing the stance, perform a right uchi-uke (inside forearm block), ensuring that the hips rotate from square on to sideways on (Fig. 95). The front knee must not move in any way during this move. It is a common mistake to cave the knee inwards during the movement.

Step 7: Sukui-uke (scooping block)

To commence the next move pull the right foot back, while at the same time pivoting right 90 degrees on the left foot so that the feet end up in heisoku-dachi (informal attention stance) facing direction 4. As the right foot is pulled back, the right hand should simultaneously be pulled back and up in a scooping action to make the sukui-uke (scooping block) (Fig. 96). At the end of the movement the right hand should be positioned so that the back of the right hand is facing away from the head.

Step 8: Migi soto-ude-uke (right outside forearm block)

The next move is a migi (right) soto-ude-uke (outside forearm block). To achieve this turn the right forearm, pivoting at the elbow, so that the back of the hand rotates 180 degrees. At the same time, push out with the left open hand (Fig. 97). This is the intermediate stage. From this point step forward with the right foot into zenkutsu-dachi (front stance) and perform a migi soto-ude-uke (right outside forearm block) (Fig. 98).

Step 9: Gyaku uchi-uke (reverse inside forearm block)

The stance remains right zenkutsu-dachi (front stance) during this move, although the hips turn to end square to the front. Commence by crossing the left arm across the front of the body while pushing the right hand forward and continue the movement to complete the left gyaku uchi-uke (reverse inside forearm block), pulling the right hand back to the hip (Fig. 99).

Fig. 100   Hikite.   Fig. 101   Tate shuto-uke.   Fig. 102   Migi choku-zuki.

Step 10: Hikite (pulling hands)
Pivoting on the right foot and pulling the left foot back, move the feet into heiko-dachi (parallel stance) facing direction 1. At the same time, move the left hand to the right hip into the hikite (pulling hands) position (Fig. 100).

Step 11: Tate shuto-uke
(vertical knife-hand block)
Without changing the position of the feet, push the left hand out to the front to make the tate shuto-uke (vertical knife-hand block) (Fig. 101).

Step 12: Migi choku-zuki
(right straight punch)
Perform a straight punch with the right hand, maintaining the heiko-dachi (parallel stance) (Fig. 102).

Step 13: Migi uchi-ude-uke
(right inside forearm block)
Pull the right fist back to the chest as a preparatory movement (Fig. 103), but do not move the shoulders or feet at this point. A common mistake is to pull the left shoulder and hip back as the right fist moves to the chest. Continue the movement by blocking the right inside forearm block, while at the same time pivoting on the feet and pulling the left shoulder backwards (Fig. 104).

Step 14: Hidari choku-zuki
(left straight punch)
The next move is a repeat of step 7, but on the opposite side. Square the shoulders back facing the front, while at the same time returning the feet to heiko-dachi (parallel stance). At the same time, perform a choku-zuki (straight punch) with the left hand (Fig. 105). The hands, shoulders and feet must complete at the same time.

Step 15: Hidari uchi-ude-uke
(left inside forearm block)
Pull the left fist back to the chest as a preparatory movement (Fig. 106), but do not move the shoulders or feet at this point. Continue the movement by blocking the left inside forearm block, while at the same time pivoting on the feet and pulling the right shoulder backwards (Fig. 107).

Fig. 103   Intermediate stage.

Fig. 104   Migi uchi-ude-uke.

Fig. 105   Hidari choku-zuki.

Fig. 106   Intermediate stage.

Fig. 107   Hidari uchi-ude-uke.

Fig. 108   Intermediate stage.

Fig. 109   Migi shuto-uke.   Fig. 110   Hidari shuto-uke.   Fig. 111   Migi shuto-uke.

Step 16: Migi shuto-uke (right knife-hand block)

The next move is right shuto-uke (knife-hand block) in kokutsu-dachi (back stance). Step up with the right foot so that your feet are together and at the same time move the right hand up to the left shoulder and push out with the left hand as shown (Fig. 108). This is the intermediate stage for this move. Make sure that you keep the knees bent so that the hips do not rise as you step. To complete the move continue to step forward with the right foot into a right kokutsu-dachi (back stance) and perform a right shuto-uke (knife-hand block) (Fig. 109).

Step 17: Hidari shuto-uke (left knife-hand block)

The next move is another shuto-uke (knife-hand block) in kokutsu-dachi (back stance). This time step up and through with the left foot into a left kokutsu-dachi (back stance) and perform a left shuto-uke (knife-hand block) (Fig. 110).

Step 18: Migi shuto-uke (right knife-hand block)

The next move is another shuto-uke (knife-hand block) in kokutsu-dachi (back stance). This time step up and through with the right foot into a right kokutsu-dachi (back stance) and perform a right shuto-uke (knife-hand block) (Fig. 111).

Step 19: Hidari shuto-uke (left knife-hand block)

The next move is another left shuto-uke (knife-hand block), but on this occasion the movement is backward in kokutsu-dachi (back stance). Step back and through with the right foot into a left kokutsu-dachi (back stance) and perform a left shuto-uke (knife-hand block) (Fig. 112).

Step 20: Migi tsukami-uke (grasping block)

Move the back foot across to the right to form a zenkutsu-dachi (front stance) at a 45-degree angle to face direction 1a. At the same time, the right hand must raise palm upward with the left

Fig. 112   Hidari shuto-uke.   Fig. 113   Intermediate stage.   Fig. 114   Intermediate stage.

hand palm down, covering the right wrist (Fig. 113). From this position, rotate the right hand so that the palm ends facing away, while at the same time moving the left hand so that the palm is facing the right forearm with the second finger positioned at the indentation made where the thumb meets the wrist (Figs 114 and 115).

Step 21: Gedan-kesage
(downward kick)
Keeping the hands where they are, raise the right knee so that it is brought up into the triangle formed by the arms (Fig. 116). Then kick downward while at the same time pulling the hands as fists back to the waist (Fig. 117) and kiai.

Step 22: Hidari shuto-uke
(left knife-hand block)
Raise the knee back up slightly after the gedan-kesage of the previous move, while at the same time turning the head to the rear (direction 3) and moving the hands to the preparatory position for the knife-hand block (Fig. 118). This is the

Fig. 115   Tsukami-uke.

Fig. 116   Intermediate stage.

Fig. 117   Gedan-kesage.

Fig. 118   Intermediate stage.

Fig. 119   Hidari shuto-uke.

Fig. 120   Hidari shuto-uke.

Fig. 121   Migi shuto-uke.

intermediate stage. From there step down with the right foot into a kokutsu-dachi (back stance) and block the left shuto-uke (knife-hand block) (Figs 119 and 120).

Step 23: Migi shuto-uke
(right knife-hand block)

The next move is right shuto-uke (knife-hand block) in kokutsu-dachi (back stance). Step up with the right foot so that your feet are together and at the same time move the right hand up to the left shoulder and push out with the left hand. This is the halfway stage for this move. Make sure that you keep the knees bent so that the hips do not rise as you step. To complete the move, continue to step forward with the right foot into a right kokutsu-dachi (back stance) and perform a right shuto-uke (knife-hand block) (Figs 121 and 122).

Step 24: Morote-age-uke
(double upper rising block)

Pull the right foot back into heisoku-dachi (informal attention stance), while at the same time

pulling the open hands back to the stomach (Figs 123 and 124). This is the intermediate stage. Then continue to raise the hands up the body so that the palms are facing inward (Fig. 125). Once the hands have reached the forehead start to clench the fists and rotate the forearms to complete the double morote-age-uke (upper rising block) (Figs 126 and 127).

Step 25: Hiza-geri (knee kick)

Raise the right knee and at the same time sharply part the fists above the head (Figs 128 and 129).

Step 26: Tetsui-hasami-uchi
(double hammer fist strike)

Step forward with the right foot into a zenkutsu-dachi (front stance) and at the same time strike inward with both fists (Figs 130 and 131).

Step 27: Migi oi-zuki
(right straight punch)

Drive forward with the right foot, maintaining a zenkutsu-dachi (front stance) and punch right oi-zuki (straight punch) (Figs 132 and 133).

Fig. 122   Migi shuto-uke.

Fig. 123   Intermediate stage.

Fig. 124   Intermediate stage.

Fig. 125   Intermediate stage.

Fig. 126   Morote-age-uke.

Fig. 127   Morote-age-uke.

Fig. 128   Hiza-geri.

Fig. 129   Hiza-geri.

Fig. 130   Tetsui-hasami-uchi.

Fig. 131   Tetsui-hasami-uchi.   Fig. 132   Migi oi-zuki.   Fig. 133   Migi oi-zuki.

Step 28: Hidari shuto-uchi (left knife-hand strike)/migi age-uke (right upper rising block)

Step across with the left foot, at the same time blocking the gedan-shuto-uke (lower-level knife-hand block) with the left hand and raising the right hand to the age-uke (upper rising block) position above the head, with the hand open (Fig. 134).

Step 29: Gedan-shuto-uke (lower-level knife-hand strike)/nagashi-uke (flowing block)

Rotate the hips and strike downward with the right-hand gedan-shuto-uchi (lower-level knife-hand strike) and palm across the front of the body to the right shoulder, with the left hand making a nagashi-uke (palm block) (Fig. 135). This move must end in zenkutsu-dachi (front stance) facing direction 1.

Step 30: Manji-uke (vortex block)

In the next movement the stance changes from zenkutsu-dachi (front stance) to heisoku-dachi (informal attention stance). This is done by pulling the left foot up to the right. As the feet move block mange-uke with the hands, which is a gedan-barai (lower-level block) with the left hand and a jodan block with the right hand, which follows a similar movement to uchi-uke (inside forearm block) (Fig. 136).

Step 31: Migi fumikomi (stamping kick)/migi gedan-barai (downward block)

The next movement is a right fumikomi (stamping kick) and right gedan-barai (downward block). At the end of the last move your body will be facing direction 4. At the end of this move the body should be facing direction 2 in kiba-dachi (horse-riding stance), but the fumikomi and gedan-barai are done in direction 1. To achieve this, the left foot must pivot on the spot until it is facing direction 2.

While pivoting on the left foot raise the right knee and the right hand in preparation for the fumikomi and gedan-barai (Fig. 137). This is the

Fig. 134   Shuto-uke/age-uke.

Fig. 135   Shuto-uke/nagashi-uke.

Fig. 136   Manji-uke.

Fig. 137   Intermediate stage.

Fig. 138   Fumikomi/gedan-barai.

Fig. 139   Intermediate stage.

Fig. 140   Haishu-uke.

Fig. 141   Haishu-uke.

halfway stage. To complete the move stamp down with the right foot and at the same time perform the gedan-barai (Fig. 138).

Step 32: Hidari haishu-uke (left back of hand block)

Turn the head to the left so that you are looking in direction 3 and at the same time cross the arms in front of the body, with the left arm underneath and the back of both hands facing up. Both fists must remain clenched to this stage (Fig. 139). Then move the left arm out slowly to the side until it is locked straight, opening the left hand as you do so. The hand must end up so that it is vertical with the back of the hand facing direction 4. This technique is haishu-uke (back of the hand block) (Figs 140 and 141).

Step 33: Mikazuki-geri (crescent kick)/mae-empi-uchi (front elbow strike)

Keeping the left hand where it is the next move involves a mikazuki-geri (crescent kick) kick to the hand (Figs 142 and 143), followed by an

Fig. 142   Mikazuki-geri.

Fig. 143   Mikazuki-geri.   Fig. 144   Mae-empi-uchi.   Fig. 145   Mae-empi-uchi.

empi-uchi (elbow strike). The supporting foot must rotate 180-degrees so that the body ends facing direction 4 (Figs 144 and 145).

Step 34: Migi gedan-barai (right downward block)

Without changing the stance, block gedan-barai (downward block) with the right arm (Fig. 146).

Note: The position of the left arm should have the fist in contact with the centre of right the upper arm.

Step 35: Hidari gedan-barai (left downward block)

Again without changing the stance block gedan-barai (downward block) with the left arm (Fig. 147). On this occasion the right fist makes contact with the centre of the left upper arm.

Step 36: Migi gedan-barai (right downward block)

This is a repeat of step 31, blocking with the right arm (Fig. 148).

Step 37: Yama-zuki (U-punch)

Move the hands to the left hip into the hikite (pulling hands) position (Figs 149 and 150), while turning the head to the right. This is the intermediate stage. To continue the move, punch out with both fists, keeping the back upright (Figs 151 and 152).

Note: This movement is taught so that the right foot steps out into a zenkutsu-dachi (front stance) with the feet hip-width apart. In the photographs it is demonstrated with the feet remaining in line.

Step 38: Hikite (pulling hands)

Pull the right foot back to heisoku-dachi (informal attention stance) and move the hands to the right hip into the hikite (pulling hands) position (Figs 153 and 154).

Step 39: Hidari fumikomi/yama-zuki (left stamping kick/U-punch)

Raise the left knee in preparation for the stamping kick, but do not move the hands at this stage (Figs 155 and 156). Then stamp down into a zenkutsu-dachi (front stance) with the left foot

Fig. 146   Migi gedan-barai.

Fig. 147   Hidari gedan-barai.

Fig. 148   Migi gedan-barai.

Fig. 149   Hikite.

Fig. 150   Hikite.

Fig. 151   Yama-zuki.

Fig. 152   Yama-zuki.

Fig. 153   Hikite.

Fig. 154   Hikite.

Fig. 155   Intermediate stage.

Fig. 156   Intermediate stage.

Fig. 157   Fumikomi/yama-zuki.

Fig. 158   Fumikomi/yama-zuki.

Fig. 159   Hikite.

Fig. 160   Intermediate stage.

and simultaneously punch yama-zuki (U-punch) with both fists (Figs 157 and 158).

Step 40: Hikite (pulling hands)
Pull the left foot back to heisoku-dachi (informal attention stance) and move the hands to the left hip into the hikite (pulling hands) position (Fig. 159).

Step 41: Hidari fumikomi/yama-zuki (left stamping kick/U punch)
Raise the right knee in preparation for the stamping kick, but do not move the hands at this stage (Fig. 160). Then stamp down into a zenkutsu-dachi (front stance) with the right foot and simultaneously punch yama-zuki (U-punch) with both fists (Fig. 161).

Step 42: Migi gedan-uchi-uke (right lower-level inside forearm block)
At the end of the last movement the body will be facing direction 3. At the end of this movement the body must end up facing direction 1, with

Fig. 161   Fumikomi/yama-zuki.

Fig. 162   Intermediate stage.

Fig. 163   Intermediate stage.

Fig. 164   Migi gedan-uchi-uke.

Fig. 165   Intermediate stage.

Fig. 166   Intermediate stage.

Fig. 167   Hidari gedan-uchi-uke.

the left foot pointing in direction 2. To achieve this, the left foot must step across backwards until it is in line with the right foot, while at the same time raising the right arm above the head (Fig. 162). To complete the move, rotate the hips left and transfer the weight over the left foot so that the stance become a zenkutsu-dachi (front srtance), but unusually with the feet in line and not hip width. At the same time, that the hips are rotating perform the gedan-uchi-uke (lower-level inside forearm block) (Figs 163 and 164).

Step 43: Hidari gedan-uchi-uke (left lower-level inside forearm block)

Without moving the feet or right arm, raise the left arm up above the head (Fig. 165). From this position, move the left arm down across the body

Fig. 168 Intermediate stage.

Fig. 169 Migi shuto-uke.

Fig. 170 Intermediate stage.

and just as it is about to touch the right forearm (Fig. 166), rotate the hips and pivot on the feet to turn, while performing the left uchi-uke (inside forearm block) (Fig. 167).

Step 44: Migi shuto-uke (right knife-hand block)

Turn the head 45 degrees facing direction 4a. Then step with the left foot up to the right while raising the right hand to the neck and pushing out with the left hand in preparation for the knife-hand block (Fig. 168). From this position, step out with the right foot into a kokutsu-dachi (back stance) and block right shuto-uke (knife-hand block) (Fig.169).

Step 45: Migi shuto-uke (right knife-hand block)

Without moving the hands, turn the head to the left, facing direction 1a and step backwards with the right foot into direction 3a (Fig. 170), completing in a right kokutsu-dachi (back stance), albeit facing backwards.

Step 46: Hidari shuto-uke (left knife-hand block)

Step with the right foot up to the left while rais-

Fig. 171 Intermediate stage.

Fig. 172   Hidari shuto-uke.

ing the left hand to the neck and pushing out with the right hand in preparation for the knife-hand block (Fig. 171). From this position, step out with the left foot into a kokutsu-dachi (back stance) and block left shuto-uke (knife-hand block) (Fig. 172) and kiai.

Step 47: Yame (finish position)

Pull the left foot back into heisoku-dachi (informal attention stance), while turning the body to face direction 1. At the same time, bring the hands together to complete the kata in the same position in which it commenced (Fig. 173). Step out with the right foot into heiko-dachi (parallel stance) and the usual yoi position (Fig. 174). From here, step back in with the right foot and perform a bow to complete the kata (Fig. 175).

Selected Bunkai

Steps 2 and 3: Hiza-geri/migi uchi-uke

The opening moves of the kata have a variety of different applications. In the first example provided here the move is used to defend against a lapel grab or push in which the attacker attacks the left chest area.

Fig. 173   Yame.

Fig. 174   Heiko-dachi.

Fig. 175   Rei.

Fig. 176   Shoulder push.   Fig. 177   Finger lock.   Fig. 178   Wrist grab.

In defence take hold of the attacker's fingers with the right hand. This can either be the little finger or two fingers. For this technique to work effectively the attacker's elbow must not be allowed to rise, so to prevent this happening apply pressure to the elbow with the left hand (Fig. 176). To continue the move twist the fingers back and slightly to the right, while stepping into the attacker as he goes down (Fig. 177).

A second example of the opening move is a defence against a wrist grab in which the attacker takes hold of the right wrist with the right hand (Fig. 178).

To defend, pull the attacker's arm in towards the body with both hands while at the same time kicking with hiza-geri (knee kick) (Fig. 179). Then immediately step into the attacker, smashing the forearm into the face (Fig. 180) to complete the move.

Steps 11 and 14: Tate shuto-uke/ choku-zuki/uchi-uke

Steps 11 to 14 consist of three types of move-ment. First there is a vertical knife-hand block, which is followed by a combination of straight punches and an inside forearm block. In the application demonstrated here the defence is against a strait or hooking punch to the head.

Use the tate shuto-uke (vertical knife-hand block) to defend against a punch to the head by striking the attacking arm close to the crease of the elbow (Fig. 181). Immediately counter with a choku-zuki (straight punch), targeting the solar plexus area (Fig. 182). The next move is a right uchi-uke (inside forearm block with a rotation of the hips). Use this move to parry the attacking arm across the front of the attacker's body (Fig. 183). The second counter-attack is a punch to the ribs that have been opened up by the inside forearm block movement (Fig. 184).

Step 16: Migi shuto-uke

The shuto-uke movement is repeated a number of times in the kata; in the example provided it is used to strike the neck and not as an actual block. The defence is against a straight or hooking

71

Fig. 179   Hiza-geri.

Fig. 180   Forearm smash.

Fig. 181   Tate shuto-uke.

Fig. 182   Choku-zuki.

Fig. 183   Uchi-uke.

Fig. 184   Choku-zuki.

Fig. 185   Shuto-uchi.

Fig. 186   Preparation for wrist grab.

punch to the head. As the attacker punches towards the head use the right palm to block the punch but in a way that attacks the forearm at the pressure point Lung 6 (Fig. 185). Then use the left hand to take hold of the attacker's wrist (Fig. 186) and complete the movement by pulling the attacker in as the right hand is used to attack the neck (Fig. 187).

Steps 20 and 21: Migi tsukami-uke/gedan-kesage

Migi tsukami-uke (grasping block) followed by gedan-kesage (downward kick) can be used to defend against a wrist grab. The attacker takes hold of the right wrist with the right hand (Fig. 188). To commence the wrist lock raise the right hand up high as in the kata (Fig. 189). From this position, hold the attacker's hand in place with the left hand and rotate the right hand over the attacker's wrist and start to apply the wrist lock (Fig. 191). Conclude the movement by using the gedan-kesage (downward lick) to kick out the attacker's left knee (Fig. 192). The kick can be used to hit the pressure point Spleen 10.

Fig. 187   Shuto strike to neck.

Fig. 188   Wrist grab.

Fig. 189   Preparation for wrist lock.

Fig. 190   Tsukami-uke.

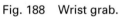

Fig. 191   Preparation for gedan-kesage.

Fig. 192   Gedan-kesage.

Fig. 193   Preparation for throw.

Fig. 194   Gedan-kesage.

Fig. 195   Completed throw.

Fig. 196   Wrist grab.

Fig. 197   Morote-age-uke.

Fig. 198   Tetsui-hasami-uchi.

Fig. 199   Oi-zuki.

Fig. 200   Haishu-uke.

Fig. 201   Fumikomi.

Fig. 202   Empi-uchi.

An alternative application for the gedan-kesage is to use it as a throwing technique in a grappling situation (Fig. 193). Raise the right knee as in the kata and kick through the attacker's leg, kicking out the front leg while rolling the upper body to complete the throw (Figs 194 and 195).

Steps 24 to 27 Morote-age-uke/ tetsui-hasami-uchi/oi-zuki

This series of movements can be used to defend against a double wrist grab. The attacker takes hold of both wrists from the front (Fig. 196). From this position, raise the arms up above the head to release the wrists (Fig. 197) and then pull the hands down and forward in a circular movement and strike into the ribs of the attacker (Fig. 198). To complete the movement, punch forward with the right fist as the attacker falls backwards (Fig. 199).

Steps 32 and 33: Haishu-uke/ mikazuki-geri/mae-empi-uchi

In this application the three moves are used to defend against a punch to the head and to counter-attack. The attack can be either a straight punch or a circular punch. Use the back of the arm to block the punch (Fig. 200). Immediately after the block take hold of the attacker's wrist and pull off balance. The mikazuki-geri (crescent kick) can be used to attack the upper leg of the knee area (Fig. 201). After the kick, follow up with an elbow strike to the face, while at the same time hitting the back of the head with the left hand. This can be used to hit the pressure points GB20 (Fig. 202).

Step 37: Yama-zuki (U-punch)

The yama-zuki movement can be used as a throwing technique in two different ways. In the first example the upper hand grabs the attacker's throat and the low hand the groin area. The throw is completed by lifting the attacker and rotating the upper body (Fig. 203). In practice, this technique would not be used against a much heavier adversary.

In the second example the throw is performed by using the upper arm to grab the clothing and the lower arm to reach under the attacker's leg (Fig. 204). Then lift the leg while rotating the upper body and throw the attacker to the floor (Figs 205 and 206).

Fig. 203   Yama-zuki as a set up for a throw.

Fig. 204   Yama-zuki as a set up for a throw.

Fig. 205   Intermediate stage of throw.

Fig. 206   Completed throw.

8 Ji'in

Kata

Step 1: Yoi (ready position)

After the bow, step out with the right foot into heiko-dachi (parallel stance) and the usual yoi position. The next movement is a step into the specific Ji'in yoi position. To achieve this move the left foot to the right into a heisoku-dachi (informal attention stance), while at the same time bringing the hands together so that the left hand encircles the right (Fig. 207). The hands must be positioned at chin height with the hands approximately 8in (20cm) away from the chin.

Step 2: Kosa-uke (double block)

Step back hip width with the right foot into a left zenkutsu-dachi (front stance), while at the same time blocking kosa-uke (double block). In Ji'in the left hand should perform uchi-uke (inside forearm block) and the right hand a gedan-barai (downward block) (Fig. 208).

Step 3: Hidari manji-uke (left vortex block)

Turn the head to the left and then step with the left foot in a circular movement forward and to the left into a left kokutsu-dachi (back stance) in direction 2 (Fig. 20). At the same time, perform a manji-uke (vortex block) with the left hand doing a gedan-barai (downward block) and the right hand a jodan ude-uke (upper forearm block) (Fig. 209).

Fig. 207   Ji'in yoi.

Fig. 208   Kosa-uke.

Fig. 209   Hidari manji-uke.

Fig. 210   Migi manji-uke.

Step 4: Migi manji-uke (right vortex block)

This is a repeat of step 3 but on the opposite side. Turn the head to the right, pivoting on the feet into a right kokutsu-dachi (back stance) in direction 4. At the same time, perform a manji-uke (vortex block) with the right hand doing a gedan-barai (downward block) and the left hand a jodan ude-uke (upper forearm block) (Fig. 210).

Step 5: Hidari age-uke (left upper rising block)

In the first part of this movement pull the left foot toward the right slightly, while at the same time turning the head and body toward direction 1a. At the same time, pull the left hand back to the hip and push out with the right hand (Fig. 211). This is the intermediate stage. To complete the move, slide forward with the left foot into a left zenkutsu-dachi (front stance) and block with the left-hand age-uke (upper rising block) (Fig. 212).

Fig. 211   Intermediate stage.

Fig. 212   Hidari age-uke.

Fig. 213   Single oi-zuki.

Fig. 214   Intermediate stage.

Fig. 215   Migi age-uke.

Fig. 216   Hidari oi-zuki.

Step 6: Single oi-zuki
(single stepping punch)

The next movement is a single oi-zuki (stepping punch) sliding forward with the right foot into right zenkutsu-dachi (front stance) in direction 1a (Fig. 213).

Step 7: Migi age-uke
(right upper rising block)

In the first part of this movement pull the right foot towards the left slightly, while turning the head and body toward direction 4a. At the same time, pull the right hand back to the hip and push out with the left hand (Fig. 214). This is the intermediate stage. To complete the move, slide forward with the right foot into a left zenkutsu-dachi (front stance) and block with the right hand age-uke (upper rising block) (Fig. 215).

Step 8: Hidari oi-zuki
(left stepping punch)

The next movement is a single oi-zuki (stepping punch) sliding forward with the left foot into left zenkutsu-dachi (front stance) in direction 4a (Fig. 216).

Step 9: Hidari gedan-barai
(left downward block)

The next movement is a gedan-barai (downward block), in which the left foot slides across to the left so that the feet end up hip-width apart in a left zenkutsu-dachi (front stance) facing direction 1 and the left hand performs the gedan-barai. Start by turning the head to direction 1, while at the commence the foot movement and move the left hand up to the right shoulder and push out with the right hand. This is the halfway stage. Continue the movement by stepping fully across with the left foot into the zenkutsu-dachi and block left gedan-barai (Fig. 217).

Step 10: Migi shuto-uchi
(right knife-hand strike)

The next three moves are completed in kiba-dachi (horse-riding stance).

From the gedan-barai position start to move the rear foot forward, while at the same time opening both hands with the palms facing down. Continue the movement with the right foot while pivoting only on the left foot, ending in kiba-dachi (horse-riding stance) so that the upper

Fig. 217   Hidari gedan-barai.

body is facing direction 2. The head should remain facing direction 1. As the feet complete the movement into the kiba-dachi (horse-riding stance), strike shuto-uchi (knife-hand strike) with the right hand, while at the same time pulling the left hand back to the hip as a fist (Fig. 218).

Step 11: Hidari shuto-uchi (left knife-hand strike)

Start the next movement by moving the rear foot forward, while at the same time opening both hands with the palms facing down. Continue the movement with the left foot ending in kiba-dachi (horse-riding stance) so that the upper body is facing direction 4. The head should remain facing direction 1. As the feet complete the movement into the kiba-dachi (horse-riding stance), strike shuto-uchi (knife-hand strike) with the left hand, while at the same time pulling the right hand back to the hip as a fist (Fig. 219).

Fig. 218   Migi shuto-uchi.

Fig. 219   Hidari shuto-uchi.

Fig. 220   Migi shuto-uchi.

Fig. 221   Kakiwake-uke.

Fig. 222   Intermediate stage.

Step 12: Migi shuto-uchi (right knife-hand strike)

Step 12 is a repeat of step 11.

The upper body must complete the movement in kiba-dachi (horse-riding stance), facing direction 2 with the head remaining facing direction 1. As the feet complete the movement into the kiba-dachi (horse-riding stance), strike shuto-uchi (knife-hand strike) with the right hand while at the same time pulling the left hand back to the hip as a fist and kiai (Fig. 220).

Step 13: Kakiwake-uke (wedge block)

At the completion of step 12 you will be facing direction 1. At the completion of this next move you will end facing direction 3A. Commence by sliding the left foot across in the direction the heel of the rear foot is pointing, while at the same time looking over the left shoulder and crossing the arms in front of the body, with the left arm in front (Figs 221 and 222). This is the halfway stage. Continue the movement by rotating the hips and upper body and transferring the weight over the left foot, making a zenkutsu-dachi (front

Fig. 223   Kakiwake-uke.

83

Fig. 224   Mae-geri jodan.

Fig. 225   Mae-geri jodan.

Fig. 226   Migi oi-zuki.

Fig. 227   Migi oi-zuki.

Fig. 228   Hidari gyaku-zuki.

Fig. 229   Hidari gyaku-zuki.

stance). At the same time, rotate the arms to perform the kakiwake-uke (wedge block) (Figs 221 and 223).

Step 14: Mae-geri jodan (front kick)
Without moving the hand position, kick right mae-geri jodan (front kick to head height), making sure that the foot snaps quickly in this kick (Figs 224 and 225).

Step 15: Migi oi-zuki (right stepping punch)
Immediately after the kick, step forward with the right foot into a long zenkutsu-dachi (front stance) and punch right oi-zuki chudan (straight punch to stomach height) (Figs 226 and 227). It is important that the punching hand is not pulled back to the hip in this punch, but instead moves straight forward from the kakiwake-uke (wedge block) position.

Step 16: Hidari gyaku-zuki (left reverse punch)

Without moving the feet or changing the stance, immediately punch left gyaku-zuki chudan (reverse punch) (Figs 228 and 229).

Step 17: Kosa-uke (crossing block)

In this movement the right arm performs an uchi-uke (inside forearm) and the left a gedan-barai (downward block). The blocks are performed simultaneously. Without changing the stance, raise the left hand to the right shoulder and push out with the right arm. Continue with the hand movement performing the kosa-uke (crossing) (Figs 230 and 231).

Step 18: Kakiwake-uke (wedge block)

The next five movements are a repeat of steps 13 to 17, only performed in direction 2A.

Commence by sliding the right foot diagonally across to the right, while at the same time looking over the right shoulder and crossing the arms in

Fig. 230　Kosa-uke.

Fig. 231　Kosa-uke.

Fig. 232　Kakiwake-uke.

Fig. 233   Intermediate stage.

Fig. 234   Kakiwake-uke.

Fig. 235   Mae-geri jodan.

Fig. 236   Mae-geri jodan.

Fig. 237   Hidari oi-zuki.

Fig. 238   Hidari oi-zuki.

front of the body, with the right arm in front (Figs 232 and 233). This is the halfway stage. Continue the movement by rotating the hips and upper body and transferring the weight over the right foot, making a zenkutsu-dachi (front stance). At the same time, rotate the arms to perform the kakiwake-uke (wedge block) (Figs 232 and 234).

Step 19: Mae-geri jodan (front kick)

Without moving the hand position, kick left mae-geri jodan (front kick to head height), making sure that the foot snaps quickly in this kick (Figs 235 and 236).

Step 20: Hidari oi-zuki (left stepping punch)

Immediately after the kick, step forward with the

Fig. 239   Migi gyaku-zuki.   Fig. 240   Migi gyaku-zuki.   Fig. 241   Kosa-uke.

left foot into a long zenkutsu-dachi (front stance) and punch left oi-zuki chudan (straight punch to stomach height) (Figs 237 and 238). It is important that the punching hand is not pulled back to the hip in this punch, but instead moves straight forward from the kakiwake-uke (wedge block) position.

**Step 21: Migi gyaku-zuki
(right reverse punch)**
Without moving the feet or changing the stance, immediately punch right gyaku-zuki chudan (reverse punch) (Figs 239 and 240).

Step 22: Kosa-uke (crossing block)
In this movement the left arm performs an uchi-uke (inside forearm) and the right a gedan-barai (downward block). The blocks are performed simultaneously. Without changing the stance, raise the right hand to the left shoulder and push out with the left arm. Continue with the hand movement performing the kosa-uke (crossing block) (Figs 241 and 242).

Fig. 242   Kosa-uke.

Fig. 243   Intermediate stage.

Fig. 244   Intermediate stage.

Fig. 245   Migi tetsui-uchi.

Fig. 246   Migi tetsui-uchi.

Fig. 247   Hidari tetsui-uchi.

Fig. 248   Hidari tetsui-uchi.

Step 23: Migi tetsui-uchi (right hammer fist strike)

The next three movements are all tetsui-uchi (hammer fist strike), performed in kiba-dachi (horse-riding stance).

The previous movement ended facing direction 2a. At the end of this movement the body must be facing direction 4, but with the head facing direction 3. Throughout this movement the left foot pivots on the spot only and it is the right foot that does most of the movement. Commence by pulling the right foot back in direction 3, while at the same time crossing the arms across the front of the body so that the right arm is under the left (Fig. 243). This is the halfway stage. Continue the movement by sliding the right foot in direction 3, pivoting on the left foot. As the feet complete the movement into kiba-dachi (horse-riding stance), strike with the right hand tetsui-uchi (hammer fist strike) (Figs. 244, 245 and 246).

Step 24: Hidari tetsui-uchi (left hammer fist strike)

This is a repeat of step 23 on the opposite side. To achieve this, the right foot pivots on the spot and the left foot does most of the movement. Pull the left foot back in the direction the heel is pointing and to the halfway stage, where the arms cross the front of the body with the left arm under the right. Continue with the movement and strike left tetsui-uchi (bottom fist strike) (Figs 247 and 248).

Step 25: Migi tetsui-uchi (right hammer fist strike)

This is a repeat of step 23; however, the feet move in a different way, with the right foot stepping forward rather than backward as in the previous two moves. Commence by stepping forward with the right foot pivoting on the left to the halfway stage. Continue moving the right foot in direction 3 to complete the tetsui-uchi (bottom fist strike) in kiba-dachi (horse-riding stance) (Figs 249 and 250).

Fig. 249   Migi tetsui-uchi.

Fig. 250   Migi tetsui-uchi.

Fig. 251   Tate shuto-uke.

Fig. 252   Tate shuto-uke.

Fig. 253   Migi gyaku-zuki.

Fig. 254   Migi gyaku-zuki.

Fig. 255   Hidari jun-zuki.

Fig. 256   Hidari jun-zuki.

Step 26: Tate shuto-uke (vertical knife-hand block)

Commence this movement by stepping with the left foot in direction 3a, while at the same time moving the left hand to the right hip and pushing out with the right arm. This is the halfway stage. Continue the movement by sliding into a full zenkutsu-dachi (front stance with the left foot and perform a left tate shuto-uke (vertical knife-hand block) (Figs 251 and 252).

Step 27: Migi gyaku-zuki (right reverse punch)

Without changing the stance, punch right gyaku-zuki (reverse punch) on the spot (Figs 253 and 254).

Step 28: Hidari jun-zuki (left straight punch)

Without changing the stance, punch left jun-zuki (straight punch) on the spot (Figs 255 and 256).

Step 29: Migi mae-geri (right front snap kick)

Without moving the hands, kick with the right foot mae-geri (front snap kick), but at the end of the movement kept the leg up (Figs 257 and 258).

Step 30: Migi gyaku-zuki (right reverse punch)

Immediately after the kick of the previous move, step back down with the right foot into a zenkutsu-dachi (front stance) and as the foot lands punch right gyaku-zuki (reverse punch) (Figs 259 and 260).

Step 31: Kosa-uke (crossing block)

In this movement the left arm performs an uchi-uke (inside forearm) and the right a gedan-barai (downward block). The blocks are performed simultaneously. Without changing the stance,

Fig. 257   Migi mae-geri.

Fig. 258   Migi mae-geri.

Fig. 259   Migi gyaku-zuki.

Fig. 260   Migi gyaku-zuki.

Fig. 261   Kosa-uke.

raise the right hand to the left shoulder and push out with the left arm. Continue with the hand movement performing the kosa-uke (crossing block) (Figs 261 and 262).

Step 32: Kosa-uke (crossing block)
At the completion of the previous move, the body will be facing direction 3a. At the completion of this next movement, the body must end facing direction 1. To achieve this pull the left foot back while pivoting on the right foot to the halfway stage. At this point the left arm must be moved to the right shoulder and the right arm pushed out to the front. To complete the movement, continue pulling the left foot back into kiba-dachi (horse-riding stance) facing direction 1 and perform the kosa-uke (crossing block) (Fig. 263).

**Step 33: Migi gedan-barai
(right downward block)**
This movement is a single handed gedan-barai

Fig. 262   Kosa-uke.

Fig. 263   Kosa-uke.

(downward block) with the right arm while maintaining a kiba-dachi (horse-riding stance) (Fig. 264).

Step 34: Ryowan uchi-uke (double inside forearm block)

In this movement both arms perform an uchi-uke (inside forearm block) simultaneously. Commence by crossing the arms in front of the body so that the left arm is in front of the right and the backs of the fists are facing toward the chest (Fig. 265). Complete the movement by rotating the forearms at the elbows so that the backs of the hands face away and the double uchi-uke (inside forearm block) is performed (Fig. 266).

Step 35: Hidari choku-zuki (left straight punch)

Without changing the stance, punch left choku-zuki (straight punch) on the spot, pulling the right hand back to the hip (Fig. 267).

Fig. 264   Migi gedan-barai.

Fig. 265   Intermediate stage.

Fig. 266   Ryowan uchi-uke.

Fig. 267 Hidari choku-zuki jodan.

Step 36: Migi choku-zuki (right straight punch)

Without changing the stance, punch right choku-zuki (straight punch) on the spot, pulling the left hand back to the hip and kiai (Fig. 268).

Step 37: Yame (finish position)

Complete the kata by moving the left foot to the right in heisoku-dachi (informal attention stance), while at the same time encircling the right fist with the left hand to complete the salutation (Fig. 269).

Step 38: Yoi

To return to the yoi position step out with the left foot.

Selected Bunkai

Step 2: Kosa-uke

Many movements in the various kata are intended to be simultaneous block and strikes in

Fig. 268 Migi choku-zuki chudan.

Fig. 269 Yame.

Fig. 270   Kosa-uke.

Fig. 271   Manji-uke as a strike.

which both hands complete the movements at the same time or in quick succession; kosa-uke is a good example of one such move in which the uchi-uke (inside forearm block) arm performs a blocking action and the gedan-barai (lower-level block) is actually used as a punching technique. This is demonstrated in this example against a punch to the head.

As the punch approaches the head, step slightly to the side and block with the right arm. Simultaneously punch into the ribs with the left fist (Fig. 270).

Step 4: Migi manji-uke

Two examples of possible applications for manji-uke (vortex block) are provided here.

In the first example the left hand is used to block a punch to the stomach, while the right upper arm is used to punch upward under the chin of the attacker (Fig. 271).

The second example of manji-uke demonstrates the movement as a set-up for a hip throw. Firstly, block the attacking punch to the stomach using the left arm and immediately hook the right

Fig. 272   Manji-uke as a throw.

Fig. 273   Blocking a head punch.

arm under the attacker's armpit and push the hip in close to the attacker in preparation for the throw (Fig. 272). The technique can continue by throwing the attacker over the right hip.

Step 5: Hidari age-uke
In this example the age-uke (upper rising block) is actually used as a strike to the neck rather than a block. There is a basic principle in karate that all so-called blocking techniques can also be used as strikes.

As the attacker punches to the head, block the arm with a left forearm block (Fig. 273). From this point grab hold of the attacker's arm with the left hand and pull the attacker in, while at the same time striking the neck with the right forearm (Fig. 274). It can be used to strike the pressure points Stomach 9 or Large Intestine 18.

Step 10: Migi shuto-uchi
The shuto-uchi in this application is used to defend against a stomach punch and counter with a strike to the neck area. Commence the movement by blocking to punch (Fig. 275). Continue by taking hold of the attacker's arm and pulling off balance, while at the same time striking the neck area (Fig. 276). The strike can be directed at the pressure point Large Intestine 18.

Fig. 274   Forearm strike to neck.

Fig. 275   Block to stomach punch.

Fig. 276   Strike to neck using shuto-uchi.

9 Jion

The Kata

Step 1: Yoi (ready position)

After the bow, step out with the right foot into heiko-dachi (parallel stance) and the yoi position. The next movement is a step into the specific Jion yoi position. To achieve this, move the left foot to the right into a heisoku-dachi (informal attention stance), while at the same time bringing the hands together so that the left hand encircles the right (Fig. 277). The hands must be positioned at chin height with the hands approximately 8in (20cm) away from the chin.

Step 2: Kosa-uke

Step back hip width with the left foot into a right zenkutsu-dachi (front stance), while at the same time block kosa-uke (double block). In Jion the right hand should perform uchi-uke (inside forearm block) and the left hand a gedan-barai (downward block) (Fig. 278).

Step 3: Kakiwake-uke (wedge block)

This move must complete in a zenkutsu-dachi (front stance) facing direction 1a (Fig. 20). To achieve this, start to move the left foot in a circular movement towards direction 1a, while at the same time moving the arms across the chest so that the left arm is in front. This is the halfway stage. Continue to slide the left foot out in direction 1a and into a zenkutsu-dachi (front stance), while pulling and rotating the forearms down to perform the kakiwake-uke (wedge block) (Fig. 279). Note the position of the back of the hands which complete the movement facing the chest.

Fig. 277   Jion yoi.

Fig. 278   Kosa-uke.

Fig. 279   Kakiwake-uke.

Fig. 280   Mae-geri.   Fig. 281   Migi oi-zuki.   Fig. 282   Hidari gyaku-zuki.

Step 4: Mae-geri (front kick)

Without moving the hand position, kick right mae-geri jodan (front kick to head height), making sure that the foot snaps quickly in this kick (Fig. 280).

Step 5: Migi oi-zuki
(right stepping punch)

Immediately after the kick, step forward with the right foot into a long zenkutsu-dachi (front stance) and punch right oi-zuki chudan (straight punch to stomach height) (Fig. 281). It is important that the punching hand is not pulled back to the hip in this punch, but instead moves straight forward from the kakiwake-uke (wedge block) position.

Step 6: Hidari gyaku-zuki
(left reverse punch)

Without moving the feet or changing the stance, immediately punch left gyaku-zuki chudan (reverse punch) (Fig. 282).

Step 7: Migi chudan-zuki
(stomach punch)

Again without moving the feet or changing the stance, immediately punch right chudan-zuki (stomach punch) (Fig. 283).

Note: The punches of steps 5, 6 and 7 must be performed in quick succession.

Step 8: Kakiwake-uke (wedge block)

This move must complete in a zenkutsu-dachi (front stance) facing direction 4a. To achieve this, start to move the right foot in a circular movement towards direction 4a, while at the same time moving the arms across the chest so that the right arm is in front. This is the halfway stage. Continue to slide the right foot out in direction 4a and into a zenkutsu-dachi (front stance), while pulling and rotating the forearms down to perform the kakiwake-uke (wedge block) (Fig. 284).

Step 9: Mae-geri (front kick)

Without moving the hand position, kick left mae-

Fig. 283   Migi chudan-zuki.

Fig. 284   Kakiwake-uke.

Fig. 285   Mae-geri.

Fig. 286   Hidari oi-zuki.

Fig. 287   Migi gyaku-zuki.

Fig. 288   Hidari chudan-zuki.

Fig. 289   Intermediate stage.   Fig. 290   Hidari age-uke.   Fig. 291   Migi gyaku-zuki.

geri jodan (front kick to head height), making sure that the foot snaps quickly in this kick (Fig. 285).

Step 10: Hidari oi-zuki (left stepping punch)
Immediately after the kick, step forward with the left foot into a long zenkutsu-dachi (front stance) and punch left oi-zuki chudan (straight punch to stomach height) (Fig. 286). It is important that the punching hand is not pulled back to the hip in this punch, but instead moves straight forward from the kakiwake-uke (wedge block) position.

Step 11: Migi gyaku-zuki (right reverse punch)
Without moving the feet or changing the stance, immediately punch right gyaku-zuki chudan (reverse punch) (Fig. 287).

Step 12: Hidari chudan-zuki (left stomach punch)
Again without moving the feet or changing the stance, immediately punch left chudan-zuki (stomach punch) (Fig. 288).

Note: The punches of steps 10, 11 and 12 must be performed in quick succession.

Step 13: Hidari age-uke (left upper rising block)
The next movement is an age-uke (upper rising block), in which the left foot slides to the left so that the feet end up hip-width apart in a left zenkutsu-dachi (front stance) facing direction 1 and the left hand performs the age-uke. Start by turning the head and commencing the foot movement, while moving the right hand up and out in direction 1 and at the same time pulling the left fist back to the chambered position at the hip (Fig. 289). This is the halfway stage. Continue the movement by stepping fully across with the left foot into the zenkutsu-dachi and block left age-uke (upper rising block) (Fig. 290).

Step 14: Migi gyaku-zuki (righ reverse punch)
Without moving the feet, immediately punch right gyaku-zuki (reverse punch) (Fig. 291).

Fig. 292   Migi age-uke.

Fig. 293   Hidari gyaku-zuki.

Fig. 294   Hidari age-uke.

Step 15: Migi age-uke (right upper rising block)

Step forward in direction 1 and perform a right age-uke (upper rising block) (Fig. 292).

Step 16: Hidari gyaku-zuki (left reverse punch)

Without moving the feet immediately punch left gyaku-zuki (reverse punch (Fig. 293).

Step 17: Hidari age-uke (left upper rising block)

Step forward in direction 1 and perform a left age-uke (upper rising block) (Fig. 294).

Step 18: Migi oi-zuki (right straight punch)

After completing the age-uke of step 19, immediately step forward in direction 1 and punch right oi-zuki chudan (lower-level straight punch) and kiai (Fig. 295).

Step 19: Manji-uke (vortex block)

This movement must complete facing direction 4. To achieve this, the left foot does most of the

Fig. 295   Migi oi-zuki.

Fig. 296　Intermediate stage.

movement while pivoting only on the right foot. Rotating the hips backward, pull the left foot across into direction 4, while raising the left hand to the right shoulder and pushing out with the right hand. This is the intermediate stage (Fig. 296). Continue by sliding out in direction 4 with the left foot, completing the move in a kokutsu-dachi (back stance) and at the same time performing the manji-uke (vortex block) with the arms so that the left hand does a gedan-barai (downward block) and the right hand a jodan-uke (upper level block) (Figs 297 and 298).

Step 20: Kage-zuki (hook punch)
Immediately after completing the manji-uke punch, with the right fist kage-zuki (hook punch) while changing the stance to kiba-dachi (horse-riding stance) by pivoting on the left foot and transferring the weight so that it is even over both feet (Figs 299 and 300).

Fig. 297　Hidari manji-uke.

Fig. 298　Migi kage-zuki.

Fig. 299   Migi kage-zuki.

Fig. 300   Migi kage-zuki.

Fig. 301   Migi manji-uke.

Fig. 302   Migi manji-uke.

Fig. 303   Hidari kage-zuki.

Fig. 304   Hidari kage-zuki.

Step 21: Manji-uke (vortex block)

This is a repeat of step 19 and is achieved by pivoting on the feet into a back stance facing direction 2. Commence by turning the head right, raising the right fist up to the left shoulder and pushing out in direction 2 with the left hand. From this position, pivot on the feet into a kokutsu-dachi (back stance) and perform the manji-uke (vortex block) (Figs 301 and 302).

Step 22: Kage-zuki (hook punch)

Immediately after completing the manji-uke punch, with the left fist kage-zuki (hook punch) while changing the stance to kiba-dachi (horse-riding stance) by pivoting on the right foot and transferring the weight so that it is even over both feet (Figs 303 and 304).

Step 23: Hidari gedan-barai (left downward block)

The next movement is a gedan-barai (downward block), in which the left foot slides to the left so that the feet end up hip-width apart in a left zenkutsu-dachi (front stance) facing direction 3

Fig. 305   Hidari gedan-barai.   Fig. 306   Migi teisho-uchi.   Fig. 307   Migi teisho-uchi.

and the left hand performs the gedan-barai. Start by turning the head and commencing the foot movement while moving the left hand up to the right shoulder and pushing out with the right hand. This is the halfway stage. Continue the movement by stepping fully across with the left foot into the zenkutsu-dachi and block left gedan-barai (downward block) (Fig. 305).

Step 24: Migi teisho-uchi (right palm heel strike)

Start the next movement by moving the rear foot forward, while at the same time opening both hands with the palms facing down. Continue the movement with the right foot ending in kiba-dachi (horse-riding stance) so that the upper body is facing direction 2. The head should remain facing direction 3. As the feet complete the movement into the kiba-dachi (horse-riding stance), strike teisho-uchi (palm heel strike) with the right hand, while at the same time pulling the left hand back to the hip as a fist (Figs 306 and 307).

Step 25: Hidari teisho-uchi (left palm heel strike)

Start to move the rear foot forward, while at the same time opening both hands with the palms facing down. Continue the movement with the left foot while pivoting only on the right foot, ending in kiba-dachi (horse-riding stance) so that the upper body is facing direction 4. The head should remain facing direction 3. As the feet complete the movement into the kiba-dachi (horse-riding stance), strike teisho-uchi (palm heel strike) with the left hand, while at the same time pulling the right hand back to the hip as a fist (Fig. 308).

Step 26: Migi teisho-uchi (right palm heel strike)

This is a repeat of step 24. Start the next movement by moving the rear foot forward, while at the same time opening both hands with the palms facing down. Continue the movement with the right foot, ending in kiba-dachi (horse-riding stance) and striking teisho-uchi (palm heel strike)

Fig. 308   Hidari teisho-uchi.   Fig. 309   Migi teisho-uchi.   Fig. 310   Intermediate stage.

with the right hand, while at the same time pulling the left hand back to the hip as a fist (Fig. 309).

Step 27: Hidari manji-uke (vortex block)

This step is completed facing direction 2. To achieve this, the left foot does most of the movement while pivoting only on the right foot. Rotating the hips backward, pull the left foot across into direction 2, while raising the left hand to the right shoulder and pushing out with the right hand in direction. This is the intermediate stage (Fig. 310). Continue by sliding out in direction 2 with the left foot, completing the move in a kokutsu-dachi (back stance) and at the same time performing the manji-uke with the arms so that the left hand does a gedan-barai (downward block) and the right hand a jodan-uke (upper level block) (Fig. 311).

Step 28: Jodan morote-uke (upper level augmented block)

Cross the left hand under the right arm as a

Fig. 311   Hidari manji-uke.

Fig. 312   Intermediate stage.

Fig. 313   Jodan morote-uke.

Fig. 314   Migi manji-uke.

preparatory move (Fig. 312). Then block morote-uke (augmented block), while stepping with the right foot into the left so that the feet end up together (Fig. 313). Note that the body is facing direction 1 but the arms finish at a 45-degree angle facing direction 1a.

Step 29: Migi manji-uke
(vortex block)

This is a repeat of step 27 and is achieved by pivoting on the feet into a back stance facing direction 4. Commence by turning the head right, raising the right fist up to the left shoulder and pushing out in direction 4 with the left hand. From this position, pivot on the feet into a kokutsu-dachi (back stance) and perform the manji-uke (Fig. 314).

Step 30: Jodan morote-uke
(upper level augmented block)

This is a repeat of step 28 and is achieved by crossing the right hand under the left arm as a preparatory move (Fig. 315) and then blocking morote-uke (augmented block), while stepping

Fig. 315   Intermediate stage.

Fig. 316   Jodan morote-uke.

Fig. 317   Intermediate stage.

with the left foot into the right so that the feet end up together (Fig. 316). Note that the body is facing direction 1 but that the arms finish at a 45-degree angle facing direction 4a.

Step 31: Ryowan gamae (double block)

Turn the head to face direction 1, while at the same time starting to cross the arms in front of the body with the right arm on top of the left (Fig. 317). Continue to pull the arms down to the sides to complete the movement (Fig. 318).

Step 32: Hiza-geri (knee strike)

Raise the right knee to strike hiza-geri (knee strike), while simultaneously pulling the fists back to the hips (Fig. 319).

Step 33: Gedan-juji-uke (lower-level X block)

Step down with the right foot, making a long stride, and as the foot lands immediately pull the left foot up behind the right to complete in kosa-dachi (crossed-legged stance) and perform a

Fig. 318   Ryowan gamae.

Fig. 319   Hiza-geri.

Fig. 320   Gedan-juji-uke.

Fig. 321   Ryowan gedan-barai.

Fig. 322   Ryowan uchi-uke.

gedan-juji-uke (lower-level X block) with the right arm on top of the left (Fig. 320). Keep the back upright at the end of this move.

Step 34: Ryowan gedan-barai (double downward block)

Pull the left foot back into a long zenkutsu-dachi (front stance) and simultaneously pull both arms back to perform the ryowan gedan-barai (double armed block) (Fig. 321).

Step 35: Ryowan uchi-uke (double inside forearm block)

Step up with the left foot to the right foot and cross the arms in front of the body in preparation for the double block with the left hand on top of the right. To complete the move, continue to step through with the left foot and perform a ryowan uchi-uke (simultaneous inside forearm block with both arms) (Fig. 322).

Step 36: Jodan juji-uke (upper level X block)

The next move is a jodan juji-uke (upper level X block). Step forward with the right foot into

Fig. 323   Jodan juji-uke.

Fig. 324   Hidari jodan age-uke/migi ura-zuki.

Fig. 325   Jodan nagahi-uke/chudan-zuki.

zenkutsu-dachi (front stance) and immediately thrust the arms upwards with the left arm on top to perform the block (Fig. 323).

Step 37: Hidari jodan age-uke/migi ura-zuki (left upper rising block/right upper punch)
Without changing the stance, punch out with the right fist ura-zuki (upper punch) and perform an age-uke (upper rising block) with the left arm (Fig. 324).

Step 38: Jodan nagashi-uke/chudan-zuki (flowing block/mid-level punch)
Without changing the stance, punch straight out with the left fist, while simultaneously pulling the right arm back to perform a nagashi-uke (flowing block) (Fig. 325).

Step 39: Migi jodan ura-zuki (upper level upper punch)
Without changing the stance, punch down and up with the right fist, while pulling the left fist

Fig. 326   Migi jodan ura-zuki.

Fig. 327   Intermediate stage.

Fig. 328   Hidari uchi-uke.

Fig. 329   Migi oi-zuki.

Fig. 330   Migi uchi-uke.

Fig. 331   Hidari oi-zuki.

Fig. 332   Hidari gedan-barai.

back so that at the completion of the movement the elbow of the right arm is positioned on top of the back of the left fist (Fig. 326).

Step 40: Hidari uchi-uke (left inside forearm block)

The previous step completes facing direction 1. At the end of this movement, the body must be facing direction 4. This is achieved by rotating the hips backward and pivoting on the front right foot. Start to rotate the body and at the same time move the left arm across the body and push the right arm out in direction 4 (Fig. 327). Continue with the left foot stepping in direction 4 to complete the movement in zenkutsu-dachi (front stance), while blocking left uchi-uke (inside forearm block) (Fig. 328).

Step 41: Migi oi-zuki (right straight punch)

Step forward with the right foot into zenkutsu-dachi (front stance) and punch right oi-zuki chudan (straight punch) (Fig. 329).

Step 42: Migi uchi-uke
(right inside forearm block)

Pulling the right foot back, perform a conventional turn so that the body ends facing direction 2 in zenkutsu-dachi (front stance) and perform a right uchi-uke (inside forearm block) (Fig. 330).

Step 43: Hidari oi-zuki
(left straight punch)

Step forward with the left foot into zenkutsu-dachi (front stance) and punch left oi-zuki chudan (straight punch) (Fig. 331).

Step 44: Hidari gedan-barai (left
downward block)

The next movement is a gedan-barai (downward block), in which the left foot slides to the left so that the feet end up hip-width apart in a left zenkutsu-dachi (front stance) facing direction 3, while the left hand performs the gedan-barai. Start by turning the head and commencing the foot movement, while moving the left hand up to the right shoulder and pushing out with the right hand. This is the halfway stage. Continue the movement by stepping fully across with the left foot into the zenkutsu-dachi and block left gedan-barai (downward block) (Fig. 332).

Step 45: Migi atoshi-uke/fumikomi
(downward hammer fist
block/stamping kick)

From the gedan-barai position of the previous step, raise the right knee up in preparation for the stamping kick and at the same time raise the right fist so that the fist is positioned directly above the knee (Figs 333 and 334). Then stamp down with the right foot in kiba-dachi (horse-riding stance) to perform the fumikomi (stamping kick), while at the same time striking down with the right hammer fist to perform the atoshi-uke (downward hammer fist block) (Figs 335 and 336). At the completion of this move the body should be facing direction 4, although the head is facing direction 3.

Fig. 333
Intermediate stage.

Fig. 334
Intermediate stage.

Fig. 335 Migi
atoshi-uke/fumikomi.

Fig. 336 Migi
atoshi-uke/fumikomi.

Fig. 337   Hidari atoshi-
uke/fumikomi.

Fig. 338   Migi atoshi-
uke/fumikomi.

Fig. 339   Atoshi
uke/fumikomi.

Fig. 340   Tsukami-uke.

Step 46: Hidari atoshi-uke/fumikomi (downward hammer fist block/stamping kick)

Raise the left knee up in preparation for the stamping kick and at the same time raise the left fist so that the fist is positioned directly above the knee. Then stamp down with the left foot in kiba-dachi (horse-riding stance) to perform the fumikomi (stamping kick), while at the same time striking down with the left hammer fist to perform the atoshi-uke (downward hammer fist block) (Fig. 337). At the completion of this move the body should end facing direction 2, although the head is facing direction 3.

Step 47: Migi atoshi-uke/fumikomi (downward hammer fist block/stamping kick)

This is a repeat of step 46. Raise the right knee and fist in preparation for the stamping kick

Fig. 341   Intermediate stage.   Fig. 342   Tsukami-uke.   Fig. 343   Yame.

and then stamp down with the right foot in kiba-dachi (horse-riding stance) to perform the fumikomi (stamping kick), while at the same time striking down with the right hammer fist to perform the atoshi-uke (downward hammer fist block) (Fig. 338). At the completion of this move the body should end facing direction 4, although the head is facing direction 3.

Step 48: Jodan tsukami-uke
The last step is completed facing direction 3. In this next move the technique is performed toward direction 2, although the body is facing direction 1. This is achieved by rotating the hips backward and pivoting on the right foot. Commence by rotating the hips backward and turning the body so that it is facing direction 1. The left foot has to step up at the same time. Simultaneously cross the right arm over the front of the body so that it is pointing in direction 2. The left hand remains at the hip at this point (Fig. 339). From this position, slide out into kiba-dachi (horse-riding stance) with the left foot and perform the tsukami-uke by punching out with the left fist and taking the

right arm back as if pulling on the strings of a bow (Fig. 340).

Step 49: Jodan tsukami-uke
The next move is a repeat of step 48 only on the opposite side. Commence by turning the head to the right, while at the same time dropping the right hand back to the chambered position at the hip and crossing the left arm across the front of the body (Fig. 341). From this position, perform the tsukami-uke by punching out with the right fist and taking the left arm back as if pulling on the strings of a bow (Fig. 342). The kiai is at this point.

Step 50: Yame (finish position)
Complete the kata by moving the right foot to the left in heisoku-dachi (informal attention stance), while at the same time encircling the right fist with the left hand to complete the salutation (Fig. 343).

Step 51: Yoi
To return to the yoi position step out with the right foot.

Fig. 344 Block covering head.

Fig. 345 Kakiwake-uke as a strike.

Fig. 346 Stranglehold.

Selected Bunkai

Step 3: Kakiwake-uke

Two examples of possible applications of kaki-wake-uke are provided here. The first is a defence against a head punch and the second is a stranglehold.

In the first example a punch to the head is blocked by raising both arms to cover the face, but keeping the elbows down to afford some protection to the chest and stomach (Fig. 344). Immediately after the block, grab hold of the attacker's arm with the left hand and pull off balance, while at the same time striking the neck area with the right forearm in a circular movement as per the kata (Fig. 345). The strike to the neck can be directed at pressure point Large Intestine 18.

The stranglehold application can be difficult to apply at first. Commence by sliding the right hand into the collar of the attacker's gi on the right side. The hand needs to take hold of the gi close to the neck with the palm of the hand facing outward. At the same time, grab hold of the left lapel of the gi with the left hand (Fig. 346). To apply the stranglehold pull the left hand across the body and the right forearm across the neck so that pressure is applied to the blood vessels in the neck. This will cut the blood supply to the brain and result in unconsciousness very quickly.

An alternative version is to use the same action with the hands, but instead of applying pressure to the neck dig into the throat with the forearm to apply a choke which restricts the airflow down the windpipe.

Step 24: Migi teisho-uchi

This application is against a punch to the head. Block the punch with the left forearm (Fig. 347) and immediately grab hold of the attacker's arm and pull of balance. At the same time, strike to the chin with the palm heel to complete the move (Fig. 348).

Step 48: Jodan tsukami-uke

This move can be used both as a punching technique, or in grappling as a means of locking the arm with an arm bar.

Fig. 347   Blocking head punch.

Fig. 348   Teisho-uchi.

Fig. 349   Block against chudan punch.

Fig. 350   Punch to ribs.

Fig. 351   Punch to chin.

Fig. 352   Arm bar across throat.

The first two examples demonstrate punching applications. Commence by blocking an attacking punch to the head with the left forearm (Fig. 349). Immediately take hold of the attacker's arm and pull off balance, while punching either into the ribs (Fig. 350) or into the chin or face (Fig. 351).

The arm bar application is a similar movement to the punching application, except that in the last part of the movement the left arm reaches right across the attacker's body so that pressure can be applied to the throat area. The attacker's arm is pulled across the chest so that the chest acts as a fulcrum, enabling the arm to be locked at the elbow (Fig. 352).

10 Jitte

The Kata

Step 1: Yoi (ready position)

After the bow, step out with the right foot into heiko-dachi (parallel stance) and the yoi position. The next movement is a step into the specific Jitte yoi position. To achieve this, move the left foot to the right into a heisoku-dachi (informal attention stance), while at the same time bringing the hands together so that the left hand encircles the right (Fig. 353). The hands must be positioned at chin height, approximately 8in (20cm) away from the chin.

Step 2: Tekubi kake-uke (wrist hooking block)

Start to move the left foot back and part the hands so that the right hand drops down. This first part of the movement should be fast and both hands should be palm down (Fig. 354). From this point, the movement becomes slow with dynamic tension. Continue to step back with the left foot into a zenkutsu-dachi (front stance), while at the same time rotating the hands so that the right hand moves inside of the left and then turns over so that the palm of the hand is upwards. The left hand pulls back to the hip as a fist (Fig. 355).

Fig. 353   Jitte yoi.

Fig. 354   Intermediate stage.

Fig. 355   Tekubi kake-uke.

Step 3: Tekubi kake-uke
(wrist hooking block)

This move finishes in direction 1a (Fig. 20) and should be performed slowly with dynamic tension. Commence by turning the head and starting to move half a pace in direction 1a. The left foot does a small circular movement to get to this point. In coordination with the foot movement, rotate the right hand so that the palm is facing down and at the same time open the left hand and start to move the hand in an upward direction (Fig. 356). Continue to step through with the left foot into a zenkutsu-dachi (front stance), while at the same time pushing down with the right hand and up with the left to complete the move (Fig. 357).

Step 4: Hidari haito-uchi
(left ridge hand strike)

Do not move the feet in this step, but maintain the zenkutsu-dachi (front stance). Turn the head while at the same time striking the upper

Fig. 356   Intermediate stage.

Fig. 357   Tekubi kake-uke.

Fig. 358   Haito-uchi.

Fig. 359   Intermediate stage.

Fig. 360   Haito-uchi.

Fig. 361   Intermediate stage.

Fig. 362   Migi teisho-uchi.

Fig. 363   Migi teisho-uchi.

Fig. 364 Hidari teisho-uchi.

Fig. 365 Migi teisho-uchi.

arm with a left haito-uchi (ridge hand strike) (Fig. 358).

Step 5: Migi haito-uchi (right ridge hand strike)

The next movement requires the right foot to step forward and toward the left foot into heiko-dachi (parallel stance) and then out to the side into a kiba-dachi (horse-riding stance). Commence the foot movement while crossing the arms with the left arm underneath the right (Fig. 359). Slide out to the side in direction 4 with the right foot and strike migi haito-uchi (right ridge hand strike), ending with the palm upward. At the same time, pull the left hand back to the hip as a fist (Fig. 360).

Step 6: Migi teisho-uchi (right palm heel strike)

This step must finish in direction 1. Commence by moving the right foot back towards the left, while at the same time pushing out with the left hand in direction 1 with the hand palm down and pulling the right hand back to the hip, keeping it open but with fingers half closed and with the hand palm down (Fig. 361). From this position, slide out in direction 1 with the right foot, completing the foot movement in kiba-dachi (horse-riding stance), at the same time striking teisho-uchi (palm heel strike) with the right hand and pulling the left hand back to the hip (Figs 362 and 363).

Step 7: Hidari teisho-uchi (left palm heel strike)

Start to move the rear foot forward, while at the same time opening both hands with the palms facing down. Continue the movement with the left foot while pivoting only on the right foot, ending in kiba-dachi (horse-riding stance) so that the upper body is facing direction 4. The head should remain facing direction 1. As the feet complete the movement into the kiba-dachi (horse-riding stance), strike teisho-uchi (palm heel strike) with the left hand while at the same time pulling the right hand back to the hip as a fist (Fig. 364).

Step 8: Migi teisho-uchi (right palm heel strike)

This is a repeat of step 7. Start the next movement by moving the rear foot forward, while at the same time opening both hands with the palms facing down. Continue the movement with the right foot ending in kiba-dachi (horse-riding stance), striking teisho-uchi (palm heel strike) with the right hand, while at the same time pulling the left hand back to the hip as a fist (Fig. 365). The upper body should complete the movement facing direction 2.

Step 9: Jodan juji-uke/ryowan gedan-barai (upper level X block/double downward block)

This movement must be performed in a straight line moving in direction 3. Step with the right foot past the left into a crossed-legged stance. In coordination with the foot movement, the hands must first be pulled back to the hip and then thrust upward to perform the juji-uke (X block)

Fig. 366   Intermediate stage.

Fig. 367   Jodan juji-uke.

Fig. 368   Intermediate stage.

Fig. 369   Jodan juji-uke.

Fig. 370   Ryowan gedan-barai.

Fig. 371   Ryowan gedan-barai.

Fig. 372   Intermediate stage.   Fig. 373   Intermediate stage.   Fig. 374   Jodan ryowan ude-uke.

(Figs 366, 367, 368 and 369). This is the halfway stage. Immediately step out with the left foot into kiba-dachi (horse-riding stance) and simultaneously pull the arms down to the sides to perform a gedan-barai (downward block) with both arms (Figs 370 and 371).

Step 10: Jodan ryowan ude-uke (upper level forearm block with both arms)

This movement continues from the last in direction 3. Step up with the right foot to the left so that the feet are together, while at the same time crossing the arms with the right arm in front of the left (Figs 372 and 373). This is the halfway stage. Immediately step out with the left foot into kiba-dachi (horse-riding stance) and simultaneously pull the arms up to perform the upper forearm block (Figs 374 and 375).

Step 11: Hidari fumikomi/jodan ude-uke (left stamping kick and left upper forearm block)

This next movement is a stamping kick with the

Fig. 375   Jodan ryowan ude-uke.

Fig. 376   Intermediate stage.

Fig. 377   Hidari fumikomi/jodan ude-uke.

Fig. 378   Migi fumikomi/jodan ude-uke.

left leg and an upper level block with the left forearm. The right foot only pivots on the spot so that the body rotates 180 degrees, ending up facing direction 4. Raise the left knee and immediately pivot on the right foot without changing the position of the arms (Fig. 376). From this position, stamp down in direction 1 and move the left hand slightly in front of the body to complete the block and kick (Fig. 377). The stance at the end of this movement is kiba-dachi (horse-riding stance).

Step 12: Migi fumikomi/jodan ude-uke (right stamping kick and right upper forearm block

This movement is the same as step 11, but on the opposite side. The left foot pivots on the spot so that the body rotates 180 degrees, ending up facing direction 2. Raise the right knee and immediately pivot on the left foot without changing the position of the arms. From this position, stamp down in direction 1 and move the right hand slightly in front of the body to complete

the block and kick (Fig. 378). The stance at the end of this movement is kiba-dachi (horse-riding stance).

Step 13: Hidari fumikomi/jodan ude-uke (left stamping kick and left upper forearm block

This movement is the same as step 11, but on the opposite side. The right foot pivots on the spot so that the body rotates 180 degrees, ending up facing direction 4. Raise the left knee and immediately pivot on the right foot without changing the position of the arms. From this position, stamp down in direction 1 and move the left hand slightly in front of the body to complete the block and kick (Fig. 379) and kiai. The stance at the end of this movement is kiba-dachi (horse-riding stance).

Step 14: Ryowan gedan-barai (double downward block)

In this step, both the feet and arms must move together and both feet must move inward equal distance from the kiba-dachi (horse-riding stance) position to heiko-dachi (parallel stance). To commence, pull the feet inward, at the same time raising the hands above the head with the left arm in front of the right (Fig. 380). Then without moving the feet pull the arms downward to the sides to perform a double gedan-barai (downward block) (Figs 381 and 382).

Step 15: Migi shuto-uchi (right knife-hand strike)

Commence this move by turning the head to the right and crossing the arms so that the right arm is under the left (Figs 383 and 384). Then step out hip width with the right foot in direction 3 into a right zenkutsu-dachi (front stance) and strike shuto-uchi (knife-hand strike) with the right hand while pulling the left hand back to the hip as a fist (Figs 385 and 386).

Step 16: Morote bo-uke

Without changing the stance, drop the right hand while at the same time striking out with the left hand. In respect of both hands, the thumbs must open up in the movement (Figs 387 and 388).

Fig. 379   Hidari fumikomi/jodan ude-uke.

Fig. 380   Intermediate stage.

Fig. 381   Ryowan gedan-barai.

Fig. 382   Ryowan gedan-barai.

Fig. 383   Intermediate stage.   Fig. 384   Intermediate stage.   Fig. 385   Migi shuto-uchi.

Fig. 386   Migi shuto-uchi.

Step 17: Morote koko-dori/sagi ashi-dachi

Pull both hands slightly back toward the body (Figs 389 and 390). Then rotate clockwise approximately 90 degrees (Figs 391 and 392) and push back out in a forward direction (Figs 393 and 394). To commence the next part of the movement, rotate the arms anti-clockwise until they are horizontal (Fig. 395). From this point, continue to rotate the arms anti-clockwise and then pull back, while at the same time raising the left knee so that the movement completes on one leg with the body facing direction 2 (Figs 396 and 397). The distance between the hands does not change throughout this rotating movement.

Step 18: Morote bo-zuki-dashi

Step out and down with the left foot to complete in a left zenkutsu-dachi (front stance) facing direction 3. At the same time, thrust out with the hands, with the right hand remaining above the left (Fig. 398). This is a similar movement to that

Fig. 387   Morote bo-uke.

Fig. 388   Morote bo-uke.

Fig. 389   Intermediate stage.

Fig. 390   Intermediate stage.

Fig. 391   Morote koko-dori.

Fig. 392   Morote koko-dori.

Fig. 393   Morote koko-dori –
stage 2.

Fig. 394   Morote koko-dori.

Fig. 395   Intermediate stage.

Fig. 396   Sagi ashi-dachi.

Fig. 397   Sagi ashi-dachi.

depicted in Fig. 410, except with the arms reversed – right at the top and left at the bottom.

Step 19: Morote koko-dori/sagi ashi-dachi

This is a repeat of step 17, but on the opposite side. Pull both hands slightly back toward the body (Fig. 399). Then rotate anti-clockwise approximately 90 degrees (Fig. 400) and push back out in a forward direction. To commence the next part of the move, rotate the arms clockwise until they are horizontal (Fig. 401). From

Fig. 398   Morote bo-zuki-dashi.

Fig. 399   Intermediate stage.

Fig. 400   Morote koko-dori.

Fig. 401   Intermediate stage.

Fig. 402   Sagi ashi-dachi.

Fig. 403   Morote bo-zuki-dashi.

this point, continue to rotate the arms clockwise and then pull back, while at the same time raising the right knee so that the movement completes on one leg with the body facing direction 4 (Fig. 402). The distance between the hands does not change throughout this rotating movement.

Step 20: Morote bo-zuki-dashi

Step out and down with the right foot to complete in a right zenkutsu-dachi (front stance) facing direction 3. At the same time, thrust out with the hands, with the left hand remaining above the right (Fig. 403).

Step 21: Hidari manji-uke (vortex block)

This step must complete facing direction 2. To achieve this, the left foot does most of the movement, while pivoting only on the right foot. Rotating the hips backward, pull the left foot across into direction 2, while raising the left hand to the right shoulder and pushing out with the right hand (Fig. 404). This is the intermediate stage. Continue by sliding out in direction 2 with

the left foot, completing the move in a kokutsu-dachi (back stance) and at the same time performing the manji-uke with the arms so that the left hand does a gedan-barai (downward block) and the right hand a jodan-uke (upper level block) (Fig. 405).

Step 22: Migi manji-uke (vortex block)

This step must complete facing direction 4. To achieve this, both feet pivot on the spot, changing from a left kokutsu-dachi (back stance) to a right stance. Commence by turning the head to the right and crossing the arms so that the left arm points in direction 4 and the right arm is raised up to the left shoulder. From this position, pivot on the feet to change stance and direction, while performing the manji-uke (vortex block) (Fig. 406).

Step 23: Hidari age-uke (left upper rising block)

This step must be completed facing direction 1. Commence by turning the head left and stepping up with the left foot in preparation for sliding

Fig. 404
Intermediate stage.

Fig. 405   Hidari manji-uke.

Fig. 406   Migi manji-uke.

Fig. 407   Intermediate stage.

Fig. 408   Hidari age-uke.

Fig. 409   Migi age-uke.

Fig. 410   Intermediate stage.

Fig. 411   Hidari age-uke.

Fig. 412   Migi age-uke.

Fig. 413
Intermediate stage.

Fig. 414   Yame.

Step 26: Migi age-uke
(right upper rising block)
Step forward with the right foot into right zenkutsu-dachi (front stance) and block right age-uke (upper rising block) (Fig. 412) and kiai. In this movement, the hands must remain as clenched fists throughout.

Step 27: Yame (finish position)
This is one of the few kata that finishes facing the opposite direction form the start. This last move should have completed facing direction 3. To return to the yame and original Jitte yoi position (jiai no kame), the body must turn to face direction 1. To achieve this, pivot on the right foot and rotate the hips backward, while moving the left foot back to the right and encircle the right fist with the left hand (Figs 413 and 414).

Step 28: Yoi
To complete the kata, step out to the conventional yoi position with the left foot.

Selected Bunkai

Steps 2 and 3: Tekubi kake-uke
The tekubi kake-uke movement can be used effectively against a wrist grab, which is how it is demonstrated in this example. Commence with the attacker taking hold of the right wrist with the right hand (Fig. 415). Following the same movement as in the kata, rotate the wrist so that the attacker's arm starts to rotate (Fig. 416). To complete the move, continue rotating the wrist and pull the attacker off balance (Fig. 417). Note how the attacker ends up in a vulnerable position.

Step 5: Haito-uchi
Haito-uchi can be used as a strike to the neck, which is how it is demonstrated here (Fig. 418), or as a strike to other vulnerable areas of the body such as the nose, temple and throat.

Step 6: Teisho-uchi
Teisho-uchi is a powerful striking technique and is particularly effective because it is strong at the wrist, as opposed to punching techniques that are prone to the wrist bending on impact.

forward in direction 1. At the same time, strike out with the right hand and pull the left hand back to chambered position at the hip (Fig. 407). From this position, slide forward with the left foot into a zenkutsu-dachi (front stance) and perform the age-uke (upper rising block) with the left arm (Fig. 408).

Step 24: Migi age-uke
(right upper rising block)
Step forward with the right foot into right zenkutsu-dachi (front stance) and block right age-uke (upper rising block) (Fig. 409). In this movement, the hands must remain as clenched fists throughout.

Step 25: Hidari age-uke
(left upper rising block)
Turn and perform a left age-uke (upper rising block) facing direction 3. In this movement, the hands must remain as clenched fists throughout (Figs 410 and 411).

Fig. 415   Wrist grab.

Fig. 416   Tekubi kake-uke intermediate stage.

Fig. 417   Tekubi kake-uke complete.

Fig. 418   Haito-uchi.

Fig. 419   Block against head punch.

Fig. 420   Teisho to chin.

Fig. 421   Teisho to floating ribs.

The examples provided here are used against an attack to the head. Commence by blocking the punch with the left forearm (Fig. 419). Immediately follow up by grabbing hold of the attacker's wrist and pulling off balance while striking with the teisho-uchi to the chin (Fig. 420).

An alternative counter-attack is to use the teisho-uchi to strike into the floating rib area (Fig. 421).

11 Kanku Dai

The Kata

Step 1: Yoi (ready position)

After the bow, step out with the right foot into heiko-dachi (parallel stance) and the yoi position. The next stage is to move into the specific Kanku Dai yoi position. To achieve this, bring the hands together to the front of the body so that the tip of the right index finger covers the nail of the left index finger and the tip of the right thumb covers the nail of the left thumb. When complete, a triangle will be formed between the hands (Fig. 422).

Step 2: Kanku (look at the sky)

Keeping the eyes fixed forward, start to raise the hands slowly. Once the hands reach eye level, tilt the head backward and follow the hands until they complete the movement above head height (Figs 423 and 424).

Fig. 422 Kanku Dai yoi.

Fig. 423 Kanku.

Fig. 424 Kanku stage 2.

Fig. 425   Intermediate stage.

Fig. 426   Intermediate stage.

Step 3: Gedan-shuto-uchi (lower-level knife-hand strike)

The next movement commences with a fast parting of the hand, which must also be pulled slightly back so that the shoulder blades are squeezed tight (Fig. 425). This is the intermediate stage. Having parted the hands, bring them both down in an arc to the front of the body, striking the palm of the left hand with shuto-uchi (palm heel strike) using the outside edge of the right hand (Figs 426 and 427).

Note: When pulling the arms back at the start of this step, do not over-extend the arms at the shoulder joints so as to risk injury.

Step 4: Hidari haiwan-uke (left back arm block)

Step out with the left foot in direction 2 (Fig. 20) into a short back stance, while blocking left haiwan-uke (back arm block) (Fig. 428).

Note: The right hand does not pull back to the hip in this step, but remains positioned across the body.

Fig. 427   Gedan-shuto-uchi.

Fig. 428   Hidari haiwan-uke.

Fig. 429   Migi haiwan-uke.

Step 5: Migi haiwan-uke
(right back arm block)

Pivoting on the feet, turn 180 degrees into a short back stance facing direction 4, while blocking right haiwan-uke (back arm block) (Fig. 429).

Note: The left hand does not pull back to the hip in this step, but remains positioned across the body.

Step 6: Hidari tate-shuto-uke
(left vertical knife-hand block)

Pivoting on the feet, turn the body back to the front facing direction 1 so that the feet end in heiko-dachi (parallel stance), while at the same time pushing out with the right arm and crossing the body with the left. The right hand must complete with the palm facing up (Fig. 430). This is the halfway stage. Continue the movement by pushing out with the left hand performing a tate-shuto (vertical knife-hand block) and pulling the right hand back to the hip as a fist (Fig. 431).

Step 7: Migi choku-zuki
(right straight punch)

Perform a straight punch with the right hand, while maintaining the heiko-dachi (parallel stance) (Fig. 432).

Step 8: Migi uchi-ude-uke
(right inside forearm block)

Pull the right fist back to the chest as a preparatory movement (Fig. 433), but do not move the shoulders or feet at this point. Continue the movement by blocking migi uchi-ude-uke (right inside forearm block), while at the same time pivoting on the feet and pulling the left shoulder backward (Fig. 434).

Fig. 430   Intermediate stage.

Fig. 431   Tate shuto-uke.

Step 9: Hidari choku-zuki
(left straight punch)

The next move is a repeat of step 7, but on the opposite side. Square the shoulders back, facing the front while at the same time returning the feet to heiko-dachi (parallel stance). At the same time, perform a straight punch with the left hand (Fig. 435). The hands, shoulders and feet must complete at the same time.

Step 10: Hidari uchi-ude-uke
(left inside forearm block)

Pull the left fist back to the chest as a preparatory movement (Fig.436), but do not move the shoulders or feet at this point. Continue the movement by blocking hidari uchi-ude-uke (left inside forearm block), while at the same time pivoting on the feet and pulling the right shoulder backward (Fig. 437).

Step 11: Hikite (pulling hands)

In this next step, the hands and feet must move at the same time. Pull the left hand back to the

Fig. 432   Migi choku-zuki.

Fig. 433   Intermediate stage.

Fig. 434   Migi uchi-ude-uke.

Fig. 435   Hidari choku-zuki.

Fig. 436   Intermediate stage.

Fig. 437   Hidari uchi-ude-uke.

Fig. 438   Hikite.

Fig. 439   Yoko-geri-keage/uraken-uchi.

Fig. 440   Intermediate stage.

Fig. 441   Hidari shuto-uke.

left hip and the right back to meet the left hand in the hikite (pulling hands) position (chambered at the hip), with the back of the hand facing out, that is, so that the right fist is in a vertical position. As the right hand is pulled back to the hip, raise the right knee. As the hands and feet move, turn the head so that you are looking over your right shoulder in direction 3 (Fig. 438).

Step 12: Yoko-geri-keage (side snap kick)/uraken-uchi (back fist strike)

The next step is a simultaneous yoko-geri-keage (side snap kick) and uraken-uchi (back fist strike). Kick yoko-geri-keage (side snap kick) with the right foot, while at the same time striking with the right hand uraken-uchi (back fist strike) (Fig. 439). The arm should complete this movement slightly in front of the kick.

Step 13: Hidari shuto-uke (left knife-hand block)

Yoko-geri-keage (side snap kick) is, as its name

Fig. 442 Migi shuto-uke.

block) in kokutsu-dachi (back stance). Step up with the right foot so that your feet are together and at the same time move the right hand up to the left shoulder and push out with the left hand as shown. This is the halfway stage. Ensure that the knees are kept bent so that the hips do not rise as you step. To complete the move, continue to step forward with the right foot into a right kokutsu-dachi (back stance) and perform a right shuto-uke (knife-hand block) (Fig. 442).

Step 15: Hidari shuto-uke (left knife-hand block)

The next move is another shuto-uke (knife-hand block) in kokutsu-dachi (back stance). This time step up and through with the left foot into a left kokutsu-dachi (back stance) and perform a left shuto-uke (knife-hand block) (Fig. 443).

Fig. 443 Hidari shuto-uke.

suggests, a snap kick. So after completing the kick at step 12 the right foot must be pulled back, but do not return the foot to the floor. From this position, raise the left hand up to the right shoulder and push the right hand through to the front (Fig. 440). Both hands are open in this movement. As the hands take up their positions, turn the head so you are now looking over the left shoulder. This is a halfway and preparatory stage for the next step, which is left shuto-uke (knife-hand block). Step down with the right foot into a right kokutsu-dachi stance (back stance) and at the same time perform a left shuto-uke (knife-hand block) (Fig. 441). You should be facing direction 1 at this point in the kata.

Step 14: Migi shuto-uke (right knife-hand block)

The next move is right shuto-uke (knife-hand

Fig. 444   Osae-uke/nukite.

Fig. 445   Gedan-shuto-uke/age-uke.

Fig. 446   Shuto-uchi/age-uke.

Step 16: Osae-uke (pressing block)/nukite (spear hand strike)/kiai

Start by palming down with the left hand without moving the feet or the right hand. This is a one-handed movement making an osae-uke (pressing block). As soon as the osae-uke (pressing block) movement is complete, step through with the right foot into a long zenkutsu-dachi (front stance) and strike nukite (spear hand) with the right hand (Fig. 444). The position of the arms at this point should be such that the crease of the wrist of the left hand is positioned just above the elbow of the right arm, with the right arm resting on top of the left. The target area for the spear hand should be the centre of the body. The first kiai is at this point.

Step 17: Gedan-shuto-uke (lower-level knife-hand block)/age-uke (upper rising block)

Move the rear foot across the line of the front foot, ending hip-width distance while turning the head to look over the left shoulder. At the same time, move the left hand downward to perform the blocking technique while simultaneously raising the right arm above the head into the upper rising block position. Both hands must be open in this move (Fig. 445).

Step 18: Shuto-uchi (knife-hand strike)/age-uke (upper rising block)

From the last position pivot the feet and twist the hips, while at the same time striking right jodan-shuto-uchi (knife-hand strike to the neck) and with the left hand perform a left age-uke jodan (upper rising block). The left hand should be open in this technique (Fig. 446). Steps 17 and 18 must be performed in quick succession.

Step 19: Mae-geri (front kick)/manji-uke (vortex block)

The next step comprises two movements that must be performed in quick succession. The first is a right mae-geri (front kick) followed by manji-uke with the feet ending in kokutsu-dachi (back stance) facing direction 1.

Fig. 447   Mae-geri.

Fig. 448   Intermediate stage.

Commence by kicking mae-geri (front kick) with the right foot, without moving the hand position (Fig. 447). Ensure that the foot snaps back quickly at the end of the kick. It is essential to remain on one leg at the end of the kick. From this position, turn the head and twist the upper body toward the left, while at the same time moving the left hand to the right side of the neck and pushing the right hand out in front of the body (Fig. 448). This is the intermediate stage. To complete the move, step back with the right foot into a kokutsu-dachi (back stance) and perform manji-uke (vortex block) with the arms (Fig. 449). The hands and feet must complete the movements at the same time. The manji-ke is a gedan-barai (lower-level block) with the left hand and a jodan block with the right hand.

Step 20: Gedan-shuto-uke (lower-level knife-hand strike)/nagashi-uke (flowing block)

Step out with the left foot into zenkutsu-dachi

Fig. 449   Manji-uke.

Fig. 450   Gedan-shuto-uchi/nagashi-uke.

Fig. 451   Gedan-barai.

Fig. 452   Gedan-shuto/age-uke.

(front stance), while at the same time palming across the front of the body with the left hand nagashi-uke (palm block) and striking forward with the right hand gedan-shuto-uchi (lower-level knife-hand strike) (Fig. 450). At the end of this movement, the hips should end square to the front.

Step 21: Gedan-barai (lower-level block)

The next move is performed slowly. Pull the front foot back into teiji-dachi (T stance), while at the same time performing a gedan-barai (lower-level block) (Fig. 451). The right hand pulls back to the hip as a fist.

The next series of moves is a repeat of steps 17 to 21.

Step 22: Gedan-shuto (lower-level knife-hand block)/age-uke (upper rising block)

Commence by stepping out with the left foot and perform a gedan-shuto-uke ending with the feet hip-width apart, while turning the head to look over the left shoulder. At the same time, move the left hand downward to perform the blocking technique, while simultaneously raising the right arm above the head into the upper rising block position. Both hands must be open in this move (Fig. 452).

Step 23: Shuto-uchi (knife-hand strike)/age-uke (upper rising block)

From the last position pivot the feet and twist the hips, while at the same time striking right jodan-shuto-uchi (knife-hand strike to the neck) and with the left hand performing a left age-uke jodan (upper rising block). The left hand should be open in this technique (Fig. 453). Steps 22 and 23 must be performed in quick succession.

Step 24: Mae-geri (front kick)/manji-uke (vortex block)

The next step comprises two movements that must be performed in quick succession. The first is a right mae-geri (front kick) followed by manji-uke with the feet ending in kokutsu-dachi (back strance) facing direction 3.

Commence by kicking mae-geri (front kick) with the right foot, without moving the hand position (Fig. 454). Ensure that the foot snaps back quickly at the end of the kick. It is essential to remain on one leg at the end of the kick. From this position, turn the head and twist the upper body toward the left, while at the same time moving the left hand to the right side of the neck and pushing the left hand out in front of the body (Fig. 455). This is the intermediate stage. To complete the move, step back with the right foot into a kokutsu-dachi (back stance) and perform manji-uke (vortex block) with the arms (Fig. 456). The hands and feet must complete the movements at the same time.

Step 25: Gedan-shuto-uke (lower-level knife-hand strike)/nagashi-uke (flowing block)

Step out with the left foot into zenkutsu-dachi (front stance), while at the same time palming across the front of the body with the left hand nagashi-uke (palm block) and striking forward with the right hand gedan-shuto-uchi (lower-level knife-hand strike) (Fig. 457). At the end of this movement, the hips should end square to the front.

Fig. 453 Shuto-uchi/age-uke.

Fig. 454   Mae-geri jodan.   Fig. 455   Intermediate stage.   Fig. 456   Manji-uke.

Step 26: Gedan-barai (lower-level block)

The next move is performed slowly. Pull the front foot back into teiji-dachi (T stance), while at the same time performing a gedan-barai (lower-level block) (Fig. 458). The right hand pulls back to the hip as a fist.

Step 27: Hikite/uraken/keage/mae-empi (pulling hands/back fist strike/snap kick/front elbow strike)

From the gedan-barai (downward block) position pull the front (left) foot back, while at the same time looking to the left and moving the hands to the right hip into the hikite (pulling hands) position (Fig. 459). This is the halfway stage. You should now be facing direction 4. The next part of the movement is a left yoko-geri-keage (side snap kick) and left uraken-uchi (back fist strike), followed by a right mae-empi (forward elbow strike). Kick left yoko-geri-keage (side snap kick), while striking left uraken-uchi (back fist strike). The hand strike should complete its movement slightly in front of the kick (Fig. 460). Then step down with the left foot into a long low zenkutsu-dachi and strike right mae-empi (elbow strike) into the palm of the left hand. At the end of this movement, the back of the right hand should be facing upward and the hips square (Fig. 461).

Fig. 457 Gedan-shuto-uchi/nagashi-uke.

Fig. 458 Gedan-barai.

Step 28: Hikate/uraken/keage/mae-empi (puling hands/back fist strike/snap kick/front elbow strike)

The next move is a repeat of step 27, but in the opposite direction. Commence by stepping up with the rear (right) foot so that the feet come together in heisoku-dachi (informal attention stance). At the same time, look to the right and move the hands to the left hip into the hikite (pulling hands) position (Fig. 462). This is the halfway stage. You should now be facing direction 2. The next part of the movement is a right yoko-geri-keage (side snap kick) and right uraken-uchi (back fist strike), followed by a left mae-empi

Fig. 459   Hikite.

Fig. 460   Uraken-uchi/keage.

Fig. 461   Mae-empi.

(forward elbow strike). Kick right yoko-geri-keage (side snap kick), while striking right uraken-uchi (back fist strike). The hand strike should complete its movement slightly in front of the kick (Fig. 463). Then step down with the right foot into a long low zenkutsu-dachi (front stance) and strike left mae-empi (elbow strike) into the palm of the right hand. At the end of this movement, the back of the left hand should be facing upward and the hips square (Fig. 464).

Step 29: Hidari shuto-uke (left knife-hand block)

The next movement is a shuto-uke (knife-hand block) in kokutsu-dachi (back stance). To achieve this, pull the rear foot across and perform the shuto-uke with the left hand in direction 4 (Fig. 465).

Step 30: Migi shuto-uke (right knife-hand block)

There then follows a further shuto-uke (knife-

Fig. 462   Hikite.

Fig. 463   Uraken-uchi/keage.

Fig. 464   Mae-empi.

Fig. 465   Hidari shuto-uke.

Fig. 466   Migi shuto-uke.

Fig. 467   Migi shuto-uke.

Fig. 468   Hidari shuto-uke.

hand block), this time stepping with the right foot into a right kokutsu-dachi (back stance). The step must be at a 45-degree angle in direction 3a (Fig. 466).

Step 31: Migi shuto-uke (right knife-hand block)

The next movement is a turn in which the right foot does all the movement and the left foot only pivots on the spot. Pull the front right foot back and perform a shuto-uke (knife-hand block), with the right hand completing the movement in a kokutsu-dachi (back stance) facing direction 2 (Fig. 467).

Step 32: Hidari shuto-uke (left knife-hand block)

The next movement is a repeat of step 31, except this time it is the left foot that is moving and the left hand performs the shuto-uke (knife-hand block). Step with the left foot in direction 2a, completing the block in a left kokutsu-dachi (back stance) (Fig. 468).

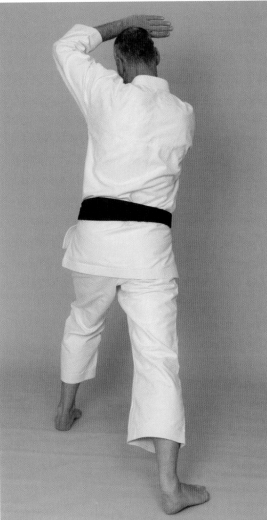

Fig. 469   Gedan-shuto-uke/age-uke.

Fig. 470   Shuto-uchi/age-uke.

Step 33: Gedan-shuto-uke (lower-level knife-hand block)/ age-uke (upper rising block)

Step to the left with the left foot so that the feet end hip-width apart, while simultaneously dropping the left hand down to the left and raising the right hand above the head to perform a left gedan-shuto-uke (lower-level knife-hand block) and at the same time a right age-uke jodan (upper rising block). The right hand should be open in this technique (Fig. 469).

Step 34: Shuto-uchi (knife-hand strike)/age-uke (upper rising block)

From the last position, pivot the feet and twist the hips, while at the same time striking right jodan-shuto-uchi (knife-hand strike to the neck) and with the left hand performing a left age-uke jodan (upper rising block) in a zenkutsu-dachi (front stance). The left hand should be open in this technique (Fig. 470). Steps 33 and 34 must be performed in quick succession.

Fig. 471   Mae-geri jodan.

Step 35: Mae-geri (front kick)/ osae-uke (pressing block)/uraken-uchi (back fist strike)

The next step comprises three movements that must be performed in quick succession. The first is a right mae-geri (front kick) followed by a left osae-uke (pressing block) and the final movement is a right downward uraken-uchi (back fist strike) done while stepping forward into kosa-dachi (crossed leg stance).

Commence by kicking mae-geri (front kick) with the right foot (Fig. 471), ensuring that the foot snaps back quickly at the end of the kick. It is essential to remain on one leg at the end of the kick. The next stage is to palm down with the left-hand osae-uke (pressing block), while at the same time raising the right hand in preparation for the final move (Figs 472 and 473). To complete the movement, step forward with the right foot the same distance that would be needed to make a zenkutsu-dachi (front stance) and immediately

Fig. 472   Osae-uke.

Fig. 473   Osae-uke.

Fig. 474   Uraken-uchi.

Fig. 475   Uraken-uchi.

allow the left foot to catch up with the right foot so that the feet end in kosa-dachi (crossed-legged stance) and strike downward with the right fist uraken-uchi (back fist strike) (Figs 474 and 475). Be sure to bring the left hand back to the hip at the end of this move.

Step 36: Uchi-uke (inside forearm block)/gyaku-zuki (reverese punch)/jun-zuki (straight punch)

From the kosa-dachi position of the previous step, pull the left foot back into a zenkutsu-dachi

(front stance) position, while at the same time performing a right uchi-uke (inside forearm block) (Figs 476 and 477). Then follow up with two punches on the spot: a left gyaku-zuki (reverse punch) (Figs 478 and 479) and a right jun-zuki (straight punch) (Figs 480 and 481).

Step 37: Hiza-geri/ura-zuki (knee strike and upper cut punch)

During this next movement, the body must turn 180 degrees and end up facing direction 1. Pivoting on the feet, start to rotate the body left,

Fig. 476   Hidari uchi-uke.

Fig. 477   Hidari uchi-uke.

Fig. 478   Hidari gyaku-zuki.

Fig. 479   Hidari gyaku-zuki.

Fig. 480   Migi jun-zuki.

Fig. 481   Migi jun-zuki.

Fig. 482 Intermediate stage.

Fig. 483 Hiza-geri/ura-zuki.

while at the same time pulling the right fist back to the hip to the intermediate stage of the move (Fig. 482). Continue to rotate the body, while at the same time raising the knee off the ground and kicking with the knee on the turn in direction 1. As the knee is raised, punch out with the right hand, with the left palm moving out to the side of the right forearm as shown (Fig. 483).

Step 38: Morote hiji tate fuse (drop to the floor)
Immediately after the knee strike and punch of the previous step, drop down to the floor in a long zenkutsu-dachi (front stance), placing the hands on the ground with the fingers pointing inwards (Fig. 484).

Step 39: Gedan-shuto-uke (lower-level knife-hand block)
Twisting to the left 180 degrees perform a gedan-shuto-uke (knife-hand block) in a low kokutsu-

Fig. 484 Morote hiji tate fuse.

Fig. 485   Gedan-shuto-uke.

Fig. 486   Gedan-Shuto-uke.

Fig. 487   Migi shuto-uke.

dachi (back stance). The left hand should end palm down and the right palm up. Note the position of the right hand, which is parallel to the upper left leg and with the hand completing the movement well in front of the left hip (Figs 485 and 486).

**Step 40: Migi shuto-uke
(right knife-hand block)**
Step forward with the right foot into kokutsu-dachi (back stance), while at the same time performing a conventional shuto-uke (knife-hand block) (Fig. 487).

**Step 41: Hidari uchi-uke
(left inside forearm block)**
In this step, the back (left) foot does all the stepping movement, with the right foot only pivoting on the spot, and it is the left hand that performs the block at the end of the move. Step across toward direction 2a with the back (left) foot and at the same time the left hand must move to the right hip, while the right hand is pushed forward

Fig. 488   Intermediate stage.

Fig. 489   Hidari uchi-uke.

Fig. 490   Migi gyaku-zuki.

(Fig. 488). Then continue rotating the hips and transfer the weight over the left foot to complete the movement in a left zenkutsu-dachi (front stance) facing direction 2. Simultaneously block with the left hand uchi-uke (inside forearm block). The right hand must be pulled back to the right hip (Fig. 489).

Step 42: Migi gyaku-zuki (right reverse punch)

Immediately following the uchi-uke (inside forearm block) of the previous move, punch right gyaku-zuki (reverse punch) on the spot, without changing the stance (Fig. 490).

Fig. 491   Migi uchi-uke.

Step 43: Migi uchi-uke (right inside forearm block)

Pivoting on the feet and rotating the hips, turn 180 degrees and block with the right hand uchi-uke (inside forearm block) in zenkutsu-dachi (front stance) facing direction 4 (Fig. 491).

Step 44: Hidari gyaku-zuki (left reverse punch)

Immediately following the uchi-uke (inside forearm block) of the previous step, punch left gyaku-zuki (reverse punch) on the spot, without changing the stance (Fig. 492).

Step 45: Jun-zuki (straight punch)

Immediately following the left gyaku-zuki (reverse punch) of the previous step, punch on the spot jun-zuki (straight punch), without changing the stance (Fig. 493).

Fig. 492   Hidari gyaku-zuki.

Fig. 493   Jun-zuki.

Fig. 494   Hikite.

Fig. 495   Yoko-geri-keage/uraken-uchi.

Step 46: Hikite (pulling hands)

In this next step, the left hand does not move from its position at the left hip. The right hand pulls back to the hikite (pulling hands) position (chambered at the hip), with the back of the hand facing out, that is, so that the right fist is in a vertical position. As the right hand is pulled back to the hip, slide up slightly with the rear foot to shorten the stance without raising the hips back with the left foot so that both feet are pointing in direction 4 (Fig. 494). As the hands and feet move, turn the head so that you are looking over your right shoulder.

Step 47: Yoko-geri-keage (side snap kick)/uraken-uchi (back fist strike)

The next movement is a simultaneous yoko-geri-keage (side snap kick) and uraken-uchi (back fist strike). Without moving the hands, raise the right knee by pulling the right foot back and up so that the knee is pointing out in direction 3. This is the intermediate stage. Then immediately kick yoko-geri-keage (side snap kick) with the right foot, while at the same time striking with the right hand uraken-uchi (back fist strike) (Fig. 495). The arm should complete this movement slightly in front of the kick.

Fig. 496   Hidari shuto-uke.

Fig. 497   Nukite.

**Step 48: Hidari shuto-uke
(left knife-hand block)**

Yoko-geri-keage (side snap kick) is, as its name, suggests a snap kick. So after completing the kick the right foot must be pulled back, but do not return the foot to the floor. From this position, raise the left hand up to the right shoulder and push the right hand through to the front in direction 1. Both hands are open in this movement. As the hands take up their positions, turn the head so that you are now looking over the left shoulder. This is a halfway and preparatory stage for the next movement, which is left shuto-uke (knife-hand block). Step down with the right foot into a right kokutsu-dachi stance (back stance)

and at the same time perform a left shuto-uke (knife-hand block) (Fig. 496).

**Step 49: Osae-uke (pressing
block)/nukite (spear-hand strike)**

Start by palming down with the left hand without moving the feet or the right hand. This is a one-handed movement making an osae-uke (pressing block). As soon as the osae-uke movement is complete, step through with the right foot into a long zenkutsu-dachi (front stance) and strike nukite (spear hand) with the right hand (Fig. 497). The position of the arms at this point should be such that the crease of the wrist of the left hand is positioned just above the elbow of the

Fig. 498   Intermediate stage. Fig. 499   Intermediate stage. Fig. 500   Hidari uraken-uchi.

right arm, with the right arm resting on top of the left. The target area for the spear hand should be the centre of the body.

Step 50: Hidari uraken-uchi
(back fist strike)

In the next step, the left foot moves back in a circular movement into a kiba-dachi (horse-riding stance) and the left hand performs an uraken-uchi (back fist strike) in a downward direction.

Commence the step by moving the left foot backward and rotating the body so that it is facing direction 2. The elbow of the right arm must remain in contact with the left hand, but the lower right arm must raise upward as the left foot starts to move (Figs 498 and 499). This is the halfway stage. Continue rotating the body 180 degrees and slide into a kiba-dachi (horse-riding stance) with the left foot. As the foot completes the movement into the stance, strike downward with the left fist performing the uraken-uchi (back fist strike) and pulling the right fist back to the hip (Fig. 500).

Fig. 501   Hidari tetsui-uchi.

Step 51: Hidari tetsui-uchi (hammer fist strike)

The next step is a one-handed strike using the left hand. Commence the movement by pulling the left fist back to the chest; this is the intermediate stage. Continue with the movement by striking out with the left hand, while sliding slightly in the kiba-dachi (horse-riding stance) equally with both feet (Fig. 501) in direction 1.

Step 52: Empi-uchi (elbow strike)

Remaining in kiba-dachi (horse-riding stance) pull the left hand back and strike the palm of the hand with the right elbow performing a mawashi-empi-uchi (roundhouse elbow strike) (Fig. 502). The head remains facing the left at this stage.

Step 53: Hikite (pulling hands)

Maintaining the kiba-dachi (horse-riding stance) position move both hands to the left hip as fists into the hikite (pulling hands) position (Fig. 503). During this movement the head must turn sharply right.

Fig. 502   Empi-uchi.

Fig. 503   Hikite.

Fig. 504　Gedan-barai.　　　　Fig. 505　Intermediate stage.　　　Fig. 506　Fumikomi/mawashi-
uke.

Step 54: Gedan-barai (lower-level block)

Without changing the stance or head position, perform a single-handed gedan-barai (lower-level block) with the right hand (Fig. 504).

Step 55: Fumikomi/mawashi-uke (stamping kick/circular block)

At the start of this next movement, the body is facing direction 4. At the end the body must have turned 180 degrees and be facing direction 2. It is the left foot that does most of the leg movement, with the right foot only pivoting on the spot to facilitate the turn.

Commence the movement by spinning on the right foot, while raising the right arm above the head and the right knee in preparation for the stamping kick (Fig. 505). This is the halfway stage. To complete the move, stamp down with the left foot to perform the fumikomi (stamping kick). At the same time as the foot lands on the ground, the arms must rotate in a circular counter-clockwise movement so that the left forearm ends waist height and the right forearm is above the head (Fig. 506).

Step 56: Otoshi-zuki (downward punch)

Without changing the stance, punch downward with the right fist so that the right arms ends on top of the left (Fig. 507).

Step 57: Jodan haishu juji-uke (open-handed X-block)

Commence this next movement by pulling both hands (as fists) back to the chest (Fig. 508). This

161

Fig. 507 Otoshi-zuki.

is the halfway stage. Both hands must then be thrust upward, opening out on the way up to complete in the X-block position. As the hands commence on the upward move from the chest, straighten both legs while at the same time shortening the stance to hip-width apart (Fig. 509), ending in heiko-dachi (parallel stance), facing direction 2.

Fig. 508 Intermediate stage.

Fig. 509 Haishu juji-uke.

Fig. 510   Intermediate stage.

Fig. 511   Intermediate stage.

Step 58: Juji-gamae (X-block stance)

This movement must be completed in a right zenkutsu-dachi (front stance) facing direction 3. To achieve this, the left foot does all the movement, with the right foot only pivoting on the spot.

Keeping the hands where they are, start to move the left foot back and rotate the body in direction 1 (Fig. 510). This is an intermediate stage. Continue to step through with the left foot in direction 1, while rotating the upper body so that the body is facing direction 3 (Fig. 511). To complete the move, slide back with the left foot into a zenkutsu-dachi (front stance) and pull the hands down into the chest (Fig. 512).

Step 59: Hidari mae-tobi-geri/ migi mae-tobi-geri/osae-uke/ uraken-uchi (left jumping front kick/right jumping front kick/ pressing block/back fist strike)

The next four movements follow in quick succes-

Fig. 512   Juji-gamae.

Fig. 513   Hidari tobi-geri.

Fig. 514   Migi tobi-geri.

Fig. 515   Uraken-uchi.

Fig. 516   Uraken-uchi.

sion. The two front kicks are performed in the air as one movement. Commence by jumping into the air, immediately kicking with the left foot followed by the right (Figs 513 and 514). On landing after the kicks, the right foot must be the leading leg; land in zenkutsu-dachi (front stance). As the feet hit the ground, block osae-uke (pressing block) with the left hand and immediately strike with a right uraken-uchi (back fist strike) and kiai (Figs 515 and 516). This movement must end facing direction 3.

Step 60: Yame (finish position)

The yame in Kanku Dai is quite a complex movement, with the body turning 180 degrees and ending facing direction 1.

Commence by rotating the body and left foot to the right, pivoting on the right foot (Fig. 517). Continue the rotation and once the body is facing direction 1 the forearms must cross at the

Fig. 517   Intermediate stage.

Fig. 518   Intermediate stage.

Fig. 519   Intermediate stage.

Fig. 520   Intermediate stage.   Fig. 521   Intermediate stage.   Fig. 522   Yame.

front of the body with the left arm on top. The left foot must then slide out into kiba-dachi (horse-riding stance), while at the same time moving the arms out to the side (Fig. 518). From this position, pull both feet in to form a heiko-dachi (parallel stance) and raise the hands in a circular movement above the head (Figs 519 and 520). To complete the movement, cross the hand in front of the body to the yame position (Figs 521 and 522).

Step 63: Rei (bow)
To complete the kata move the right foot into the left and perform the bow.

Selected Bunkai

Steps 2 and 3: Opening move to gedan-shuto-uchi
In the example here, the opening moves of Kanku Dai are used as a release against a double-handed wrist hold. Commence with the attacker taking hold of both wrists as shown (Fig. 523). To secure the release start by opening both hands so that they are palm down, as in the kata at the start of the move. This action has the effect of expanding the muscles in the forearms. From this position, start to raise the arms exactly as in the kata (Fig. 524).

Fig. 523   Double wrist grab.

Fig. 524   Intermediate stage.

Fig. 525   Wrist grab release.

Fig. 526   Arm lock.

Fig. 527   Wrist lock.

Fig. 528   Shuto strike to nose.

As the hands start to rise, pressure will be applied to the attacker's thumbs, which is the point of weakness in this hold. Continue to raise the arms until the wrist hold is released (Fig. 525). Once the wrists are released it will be possible to grab hold of the attacker's wrists; continue in a circular movement so that the attacker's forearms are twisted and the arms locked up (Fig. 526).

If the final twisting action is applied to one wrist only, the attacker's legs will bend and the body will twist as shown (Fig. 527).

This will enable application of the shuto-uchi (knife-hand strike) to the face as in the kata (Fig. 528).

An alternative application of the opening moves is to strike into the throat and neck with both open hands. In this application the thumbs should dig into the throat in the soft area just above the end of the breast bone. The bones at the base of the index fingers can attack the side of the neck at the same time (Fig. 529). The move can be completed if necessary by applying a stranglehold.

Fig. 529
Strike to
throat.

Fig. 530   Gedan-shuto-uke.

Fig. 531   Shuto-uchi.

Fig. 532   Hiza-geri.

Fig. 533   Morote hiji tate fuse.

Fig. 534
Intermediate stage.

Fig. 535
Full take-down.

Fig. 536   Jodan juji-uke.   Fig. 537   Preparation for throw.

Steps 17 and 18: Gedan-shuto-uke/shuto-uchi

These two moves are demonstrated as a defence against a stomach punch. As the attacking punch nears the body block it with the gedan-barai (downward block), while at the same time covering the face with the right hand in anticipation of a second attacking punch (Fig. 530). To counter, grab hold of the attacker's wrist with the left hand and pull off balance, while striking the neck with the knife-hand strike (Fig. 531). This strike can be to the pressure point Large Intestine 18.

Steps 37 and 38: Hiza-geri/morote hiji tate fuse

These movements can be used in a number of ways. In the examples shown here the moves are used as a pre-emptive attack, although they could be equally applied in grappling-type situations. Commence by kicking the attacker in the solar plexus area with the right knee (Fig. 532). As the attacker staggers back, drop down and grab hold of both legs (Fig. 533). To complete the move, pull both legs sharply forward until the attacker drops to the floor (Figs 534 and 535).

Steps 57 and 58: Juji-uke/juji-gamae

These two moves are used in this example as a defence against a downward strike to the head and to follow up with an elbow lock that could be continued into a throwing technique. When the attacking arm is just above the head, block with a juji-uke (X-block) (Fig. 536).

To counter, take hold of the attacker's arm and rotate 180 degrees left so that the attacker's arm is across the shoulder and the shoulder is used as a fulcrum to apply the arm lock (Fig. 537).

12 Enpi

The Kata

Step 1: Yoi (ready position)

After the bow, step out with the right foot into heiko-dachi (parallel stance) and the yoi position. The next movement is a step into the specific Enpi yoi position. To achieve this, move the left foot into the right and move the right fist across the body so that it makes contact with the left open hand at the left hip (Fig. 538).

Step 2: Migi gedan-barai (right downward block)

Step out with the left foot in direction 2 (Fig. 20), while at the same time dropping down onto the right knee and performing a right gedan-barai (downward block) (Fig. 539).

Note: The position of the left hand does not pull back to the usual chambered position at the hip but instead is positioned across the stomach.

Step 3: Koshi-gamae (fists at the hip position)

Pull the left foot back up into heiko-dachi (parallel stance), while at the same time moving the hands to the hikite (pulling hands) position at the left hip (Fig. 540).

Fig. 538   Enpi yoi.

Fig. 539   Migi gedan-barai.

Fig. 540   Koshi-gamae.

Fig. 541   Migi gedan-barai.   Fig. 542   Migi kage-zuki.   Fig. 543   Hidari kage-zuki.

Step 4: Migi gedan-barai
(right downward block)
With the right foot step out to the right in direction 4 and perform a gedan-barai (downward block) in zenkutsu-dachi (front stance) (Fig. 541).

Step 5: Migi kage-zuki
(right hook punch)
Pull the left foot back so that the feet are in line and change the stance to kiba-dachi (horse-riding stance) by transferring the weight evenly over both feet. At the same time, punch kage-zuki (hook punch) with the right fist (Fig. 542).

Step 6: Hidari kage-zuki
(left hook punch)
Immediately following the previous move, punch left kage-zuki (hook punch) without changing the stance (Fig. 543).

Note: The two hook punches must be performed in quick succession.

Step 7: Hidari gedan-barai
(left downward block)
Step in direction 1 into a left zenkutsu-dachi (front stance) and perform a left gedan-barai (downward block) (Fig. 544).

Fig. 544   Hidari gedan-barai.

Fig. 545   Migi age-zuki.

Fig. 546   Kami-zukami.

Fig. 547   Kami-zukami.

Step 8: Migi age-zuki (right rising punch)

Without changing the stance, the next move is a right jodan age-zuki (rising punch to head height) (Fig. 545). The hips must, however, rotate to the front as if performing a gyaku-zuki (reverse punch).

Step 9: Kami-zukami (hair grasp)

In this next movement the stance remains the same. The right hand performs a circular movement with a slight pull down at the end. Commence by opening the right hand (Fig. 546). Then start to rotate the hand to the left and continue in a circular direction until the palm of the hand is back to where it started at the open-hand position (Fig. 547). There should be a slight pull downward at the end of the move.

Step 10: Migi hiza-geri (right knee kick)

Without moving the hand position, move the right knee upward to perform the hiza-geri (knee kick) (Fig. 548).

Fig. 548   Migi hiza-geri.

Fig. 549   Nagashi-uke/otoshi-zuki.

Fig. 550   Migi gedan-barai.

Fig. 551   Hidari gedan-barai.

Step 11: Migi nagashi-uke/hidari otoshi-zuki (right sweeping block/left downward punch)

In this step, both feet must move in a forward direction so that they end up in kosa-dachi (crossed-legged stance) with the left shin in contact with the calf muscle of the right leg. To achieve this, the right foot steps down after the hiza-geri and the left foot slides along the floor to meet the right. As the right foot lands and the left foot starts to slide forward, simultaneously perform the migi nagashi-uke (right sweeping block) and hidari otoshi-zuki (left downward punch) (Fig. 549).

Step 12: Migi gedan-barai (right downward block)

Pull the left foot back in direction 3 into a zenkutsu-dachi (front stance) but with the feet in line, while at the same time blocking right gedan-barai (downward block), looking over the right shoulder (Fig. 550).

Step 13: Hidari gedan-barai (left downward block)

Turn the head to the left and perform a left gedan-barai (downward block), while at the same time stepping with the left foot out to the left to finish in a conventional zenkutsu-dachi (front stance) with the feet hip-width apart (Fig. 551).

Step 14: Migi age-zuki (right rising punch)

Without changing the stance, the next move is a right jodan age-zuki (rising punch to head height) (Fig. 552), which is a repeat of step 8.

Step 15: Kami-zukami (hair grasp)

This is a repeat of step 9. The stance remains the same while the right hand performs a circular movement with a slight pull down at the end. Commence by opening the right hand. Then start to rotate the hand to the left and continue in a circular direction until the palm of the hand is back to where it started at the open-hand position, with a slight downward pull at the end (Fig. 553).

Step 16: Migi hiza-geri (right knee kick)

Without moving the hand position, move the right knee upward to perform the hiza-geri (knee kick) (Fig. 554).

Step 17: Migi nagashi-uke/hidari otoshi-zuki (right sweeping block/ left downward punch)

In this step, both feet must move in a forward direction so that they end up in kosa-dachi (crossed-legged stance) with the left shin in contact with the calf muscle of the right leg. To achieve this, the right foot steps down after the hiza-geri and the left foot slides along the floor to meet the right. As the right foot lands and the left foot starts to slide forward, simultaneously per-

form the migi nagashi-uke (right sweeping block) and hidari otoshi-zuki (left downward punch) (Fig. 555).

Step 18: Migi gedan-barai (right downward block)

Pull the left foot back in direction 1 into a zenkutsu-dachi (front stance) but with the feet in line, while at the same time blocking right gedan-barai (downward block), looking over the right shoulder (Fig. 556).

Fig. 552   Migi age-zuki.

Fig. 553   Kami-zukami.

Fig. 554   Migi hiza-geri.

Fig. 555   Nagashi-uke/otoshi-zuki.

Fig. 556   Migi gedan-barai.

Fig. 557   Hidari gedan-barai.

Fig. 558   Intermediate stage.

Fig. 559   Haishu-uke.

Fig. 560   Kata ashi-dachi.

Step 19: Hidari gedan-barai (left downward block)

Turn the head to the left and perform a left gedan-barai (downward block), while at the same time stepping with the left foot out to the left to finish in a conventional zenkutsu-dachi (front stance) with the feet hip-width apart (Fig. 557).

Step 20: Jodan haishu-uke (upper level back arm block)

At the end of the last movement the body should be facing direction 1. At the end of this movement the body remains facing direction 1, but the stance changes to kiba-dachi (horse-riding stance). Commence by pulling the front foot and left arm backward (Fig. 558) and then in a circular movement step down to the left into the kiba-dachi (horse-riding stance). At the end of the movement, the head should be facing 45 degrees left. The left arm must follow the circular movement of the left leg and end up positioned so that the elbow is directly above the left knee and the hand opened (Fig. 559).

Step 21: Kata ashi-dachi (one-legged stance)

While raising the right foot so that it hooks around the back of the left knee, punch upwards with the right fist at a 45-degree angle so that the forearm makes contact with the palm of the left hand (Fig. 560) and kiai.

Step 22: Tate-shuto-uke (vertical knife-hand block)

Step back down with the right foot into kiba-dachi (horse-riding stance), while at the same time blocking tate-shuto-uke (vertical knife-hand block) with the left hand (Fig. 561).

Step 23: Migi chudan-zuki (straight punch)

Maintaining the kiba-dachi (horse-riding stance), punch in a straight line with the right fist (Fig. 562).

Step 24: Hidari chudan-zuki (straight punch)

Maintaining the kiba-dachi (horse-riding stance), punch in a straight line with the left fist (Fig. 563).

Step 25: Hidari gedan-barai (downward block)

Step across to the left in direction 2 with the left

Fig. 561   Tate-shuto-uke.

Fig. 562   Migi chudan-zuki.

Fig. 563   Hidari chudan-zuki.

Fig. 564   Hidari gedan-barai.

Fig. 565   Migi age-zuki.

Fig. 566   Migi shuto-uke.

foot so that the feet end hip-width apart in zenkutsu-dachi (front stance) and block gedan-barai (downward block) (Fig. 564).

Step 26: Migi age-zuki (right rising punch)

Without changing the stance, the next move is a right jodan age-zuki (rising punch to head height) (Fig. 565).

Step 27: Migi shuto-uke (right knife-hand block)

Step forward with the right foot into a kokutsu-dachi (back stance), while performing a shuto-uke (knife-hand block) with the right hand (Fig. 566). This movement should complete in direction 2.

Step 28: Hidari shuto-uke (left knife-hand block)

This next movement should complete in a left kokutsu-dachi (back stance), but to achieve this both feet must move. Commence by pulling the right foot back to the left so that the feet are together and raise the left hand to the right side of the neck. This is the halfway stage. To complete

Fig. 567 Hidari shuto-uke.

Fig. 568 Migi gyaku-zuki.

Fig. 569 Migi shuto-uke.

Fig. 570 Hidari gedan-barai.

Fig. 571 Migi age-zuki.

Fig. 572 Kami-zukami.

the movement, step forward with the left foot and block left shuto-uke (knife-hand block) (Fig. 567).

Step 29: Gyaku-zuki (reverse punch)
Ensuring that the stance remains unchanged, punch right gyaku-zuki (reverse punch) on the spot (Fig. 568).

Step 30: Migi shuto-uke (right knife-hand block)
Step forward with the right foot into a kokutsu-dachi (back stance), while performing a shuto-uke (knife-hand block) with the right hand (Fig. 569). This movement should complete in direction 2.

Fig. 573 Migi hiza-geri.

Fig. 574 Migi nagashi-uke/hidari otoshi-zuki.

Fig. 575 Migi gedan-barai.

Step 31: Hidari gedan-barai (downward block)

This movement is a conventional turn and downward block to the rear. Step across with the rear (left) foot to the halfway stage of the turn, raising the left fist to the right side of the neck. Continue with the turn by rotating the hips and transferring the weight over the left foot, while simultaneously blocking left gedan-barai (downward block) (Fig. 570). This move should complete in direction 4.

Step 32: Migi age-zuki (right rising punch)

Without changing the stance, the next move is a right jodan age-zuki (rising punch to head height) (Fig. 571). The hips must, however, rotate to the front as if performing a gyaku-zuki (reverse punch).

Step 33: Kami-zukami (hair grasp)

In this next step the stance remains the same. The right hand performs a circular movement with a slight pull down at the end. Commence by opening the right hand. Then start to rotate the hand to the left and continue in a circular direction until the palm of the hand is back to where it started at the open-hand position (Fig. 572).

Step 34: Migi hiza-geri (right knee kick)

Without moving the hand position, move the right knee upwards to perform the hiza-geri (knee kick) (Fig. 573).

Step 35: Migi nagashi-uke/hidari otoshi-zuki (right sweeping block/ left downward punch)

In this step both feet must move in a forward direction so that they end up in kosa-dachi (crossed-legged stance), with the left shin in contact with the calf muscle of the right leg. To achieve this, the right foot steps down after the hiza-geri and the left foot slides along the floor to meet the right. As the right foot lands and the left foot starts to slide forward, simultaneously perform the migi nagashi-uke (right sweeping block) and hidari otoshi-zuki (left downward punch) (Fig. 574).

Step 36: Migi gedan-barai (right downward block)

Pull the left foot back in direction 2 into a zenkutsu-dachi (front stance) but with the feet in line, while at the same time blocking right gedan-barai (downward block), looking over the right shoulder (Fig. 575).

Fig. 576   Hidari gedan-barai.   Fig. 577   Intermediate stage.   Fig. 578   Migi teisho-uke.

Step 37: Hidari gedan-barai (left downward block)

Turn the head to the left and perform a left gedan-barai (downward block), while at the same time stepping with the left foot out to the left to finish in a conventional zenkutsu-dachi (front stance) with the feet hip-width apart (Fig. 576).

Step 38: Migi teisho-uke (right palm heel block)

Without changing the stance, block teisho-uke (palm heel block). The right hand must end up palm upward (Figs 577 and 578).

Step 39: Teisho kosa-uke (two-handed palm heel block)

In this next movement the right hand performs a hooking action at the wrist while the left hand pushes downward to perform a pressing block. Commence the movement by stepping up with the rear foot to the halfway stage, at the same time raising the left hand palm upward and pushing down with the right (Fig. 579). From this position, slide through with the right foot into zenkutsu-dachi (front stance), while simultaneously rotating the left forearm so that the hand pushes downward and to the right so that the hand hooks over with the palm of the hand finishing palm upward (Fig. 580).

Step 40: Teisho kosa-uke (two-handed palm heel block)

This movement is a repeat of step 39, but on the opposite side. Step through with the left foot into a zenkutsu-dachi (front stance), simultaneously pushing down with the right hand and hooking over with the palm of the left hand finishing palm upwards (Fig. 581).

Step 41: Teisho kosa-uke (two-handed palm heel block)

This movement is a repeat of step 39. Step through with the right foot into a zenkutsu-dachi (front stance), simultaneously pushing down with the left hand and hooking over with the palm of the right hand finishing palm upwards (Fig. 582).

Step 42: Migi gedan-barai (downward block)

This step requires a change of stance on the spot into kokutsu-dachi (back stance). To do this, slide the right foot to the left so that the feet end up with the heels of the feet in line and 70 per cent

Fig. 579   Intermediate stage.

Fig. 580   Teisho kosa-uke.

Fig. 581   Teisho kosa-uke.

Fig. 582   Teisho kosa-uke.

Fig. 583   Migi gedan-barai.

Fig. 584   Morote koko-
gamae.

of the weight transferred to the rear foot. At the same time, perform a gedan-barai (downward block) (Fig. 583).

Step 43: Morote koko-gamae (double-handed tiger mouth grasp)
Slide forward slightly into kiba-dachi (horse-riding stance) and reach out with both hands in a grabbing-type movement, with the right hands palm upward at groin height and the left hand head height, also palm upwards (Fig. 584).

Step 44: Migi shuto-uke (right knife-hand block)
This step commences facing direction 1 and should conclude facing the same direction but

183

Fig. 585 Intermediate stage.

Fig. 586 Migi shuto-uke.

Fig. 587 Hidari shuto-uke.

Fig. 588 Yame.

after a jump of 360 degrees. Moving in a circular movement to the left, launch the body into the air and whilst in the air move the right hand to the left shoulder in preparation for the knife-hand block. After the turn, land in a migi kokutsu-dachi (right back stance) and perform a right shuto-uke (knife-hand block) (Figs 585 and 586).

Step 45: Hidari shuto-uke (left knife-hand block)

The next movement is a step backward into a left kokutsu-dachi (back stance), while at the same time performing a left shuto-uke (knife-hand block) (Fig. 587).

Step 46: Yame (finish position)

To conclude the kata, pull the left foot back into heisoku-dachi (parallel stance) and move the hands to the left hip in the same position that the kata commenced, as described at step 1 above (Fig. 588). From this position, step out with the right foot to the conventional yoi position and then conclude with a bow by moving the right foot back into the left.

Fig. 589 Defence from the ground.

Selected Bunkai

Step 2 Migi gedan-barai

Fig. 590   Wrist grab.

Fig. 591   Off-balancing move.

Fig. 592   Drop to the knee.

Fig. 593   Take-down.

Fig. 594   Block against stomach punch.

Fig. 595   Age-zuki.

The first example of the gedan-barai move that opens the kata is used as a defence from a ground position. In the scenario depicted it is envisaged that the defender is pinning down one attacker on the floor, while another attempts to kick. The gedan-barai defends against the incoming kick (Fig. 589).

In the second example the move is used against a wrist grab. Commence with the attacker taking hold of the right wrist with the right hand (Fig. 590). From this position, pull the attacker's hand back to the right hip following the hikite (pulling hands) move from within the kata (Fig. 591). This will off-balance the attacker. From this position, drop down onto the right knee in preparation for the take-down (Fig. 592). To complete the move, hook the right arm under the attacker's leg and lift to effect the take-down (Fig. 593).

Fig. 596   Hair grab.

Step 8: Migi age-zuki

Age-zuki is a rising punch that can be deceptive and difficult to block or defend against. In this example it is used following a block of a stomach punch (Fig. 594). The age-zuki commences from the hip and gradually rises through its forward movement, ultimately punching the chin and face area (Fig. 595).

Steps 9 and 10: Kami-zukami/hiza-geri

Kami-zukami is a hair grab. When the kata was created it must be remembered that the top knot was common and this provided a good means of controlling the head if it could be taken hold of. Even without the top knot the move still has a modern-day application. It can be used to grab the hair if the attacker has long enough hair, or alternatively clothing such as hooded tops. In this example it is used to pull the hair. Grab the hair at the back (Fig. 596) and rotate the hand as in the kata and pull downward to take control of the head (Fig. 597). Complete the move by kicking hiza-geri with the knee (Fig. 598).

Fig. 597   Controlling the head.

Fig. 598   Hiza-geri.

Notes

Chapter 2

1. www.shaolin-society.co.uk.
2. www.home.vtmuseum.org/articles/meng/ holy_land.php (accessed 30/8/2008).
3. www.mts.net/~sillum/South%20Shaolin% 20Temple1.htm (accessed 30/8/2008).
4. Ying Zi and Weng Yi, *Shaolin Kung Fu*, pp.8–9.
5. *Sports and Games of Ancient China* (New World Press, Beijing), p.5.
6. Bonnefoy, Yves (1993), *Asian Mythologies* (translated by Wendy Doniger) (University of Chicago Press), p.246.
7. P.Y. Ho and F.P. Lisowski, *A Brief History of Chinese Medicine and its Influence*, p.13.
8. Ki Tianji and Du Xilian, *A Guide to Chinese Martial Arts*, p.3.
9. *Sports and Games of Ancient China* (New World Press, Beijing), p. 97.
10. Ying Zi and Weng Yi, *Shaolin Kung Fu*, p.11.
11. Ki Tianji and Du Xilian, *A Guide to Chinese Martial Arts*, p.3.
12. *Sport and Games of Ancient China*, p.109 (New World Press, Beijing).
13. *Sport and Games of Ancient China*, p.105 (New World Press, Beijing).
14. Ying Zi and Weng Yi, *Shaolin Kung Fu*, p.141.
15. *Sports and Games of Ancient China*, p. 97 (New World Press, Beijing).

16. Ki Tianji and Du Xilian, *A Guide to Chinese Martial Arts*, p.6.
17. Ki Tianji and Du Xilian, *A Guide to Chinese Martial Arts*, pp.3–4.
18. *Sports and Games in Ancient China* (New World Press, Beijing), p.5.
19. Dr Yang, Jwing-Ming, *The Essence of Shaolin White Crane*, p.5.
20. Dr Yang, Jwing-Ming, *The Essence of Shaolin White Crane*, p.4.
21. *Sport and Games in Ancient China* (New World Press, Beijing), p.101.
22. *Sport and Games in Ancient China* (New World Press, Beijing), pp.22–3.

Chapter 4

23. Gichin Funakoshi, *Karate-do Kyohan*, p.227.
24. Patrick McCarthy, *Classical Kata of Okinawan Karate*, p.57.
25. Patrick McCarthy, *Classical Kata of Okinawan Karate*, p.57.
26. *Karate Do My Way of Life*, p.105.
27. Gichin Funakoshi, *Karate-do Kyohan*, p. 39.

Chapter 5

28. Gichin Funakoshi, *Karate-do Kyohan*, p.35.
29. Shoshin Nagamine, *The Essence of Okinawan Karate-do*, p.116.

Bibliography and Further Reading

Bishop, M., *Zen Kobudo* (Tuttle Publishing, 1996)

Bishop, M., *Okinawan Karate: Teachers, Styles and Secret Techniques* (A & C Black, 1989)

Clark, R., *Pressure Point Fighting: A Guide to the Secret Heart of Asian Martial Arts* (Tuttle Publishing, 2000)

Croft, A., *Shotokan Karate* (The Crowood Press, 2001)

Croft, A., *Secret Karate: The Hidden Pressure Point Techniques of Karate Kata* (The Crowood Press, 2003)

Croft, A., *Shotokan Karate: Unravelling the Kata* (The Crowood Press, 2006)

Demura, F., Bo, *Karate Weapon of Self Defence* (Ohara Publications, 1989)

Funakoshi, G., *Karate-do Nyumon* (Kodansha, 1987)

Funakoshi, G., *Karate-do My Way of Life* (Kodansha, 1975)

Funakoshi, G., *To-te Jitsu and Gichin Funakoshi – Karate-do Kyohan* (Masters Publication, 1997)

Haines, B., *Karate History and Traditions* (Tuttle Publishing, 1968)

Hall, B., *Account of the Voyage to China, Corea and Loo Choo 1816* (Hall, 1816)

Kerr, *Okinawa, The History of an Island People* (Tuttle, 2000)

McCarthy, P., *Classical Kata of Okinawan Karate* (Ohara Publications, 1987)

McCarthy, P., *The Bible of Karate: Bubishi* (Tuttle Publishing, 1995)

McCarthy, P., *Ancient Okinawan Martial Arts: Koryu Uchinada 2* (Tuttle Publishing, 1999)

McLeod, J., *Voyage of the Alceste* (McLeod, 1816)

Nagamine, S., *Tales of Okinawa's Great Masters* (Translated by Patrick McCarthy) (Tuttle Publishing, 2000)

The Bishop of Victoria, *The Bishop of Victoria's visit to Lewchew* (1850)

Index